John C. King

A Christian View
of the Mushroom Myth

HODDER AND STOUGHTON
LONDON · SYDNEY · AUCKLAND · TORONTO

Contents

Mushroom or milestone?

When I first read Mr Allegro's book *The Sacred Mushroom and the Cross* I had never heard of the fly agaric, or *amanita muscaria*. If I had seen a specimen I should probably have described it as a toadstool – which only serves to show how loosely we handle plant-names, particularly those of us who have difficulty in distinguishing hedge-parsley from hog-weed. I had, and still have, difficulty in taking Mr Allegro seriously; his book is ingenious, infuriating and occasionally amusing but it makes the most enormous demands on the credulity of the reader. Not many people are likely to be seriously disturbed by a fantasy so egregious, but Mr Allegro wishes us to give serious consideration to his views and the effort must be made. There is one good reason for making this effort. To my certain knowledge there are schoolboys who confront their R.E. teacher with the mushroom theory just as a few weeks or months before there were schoolboys who confronted him with the theory that God is an astronaut. Perhaps there are others who have heard about the sacred mushroom but have not noticed what scholars have said about it. Scholars are not accustomed to claiming attention amongst the populace at large and something of a popular rebuttal of Mr Allegro's fanciful idea may therefore be in order. If Mr Allegro is right, people who have put their faith in Christ have fallen for a figment of somebody else's imagination. I am sure that I am not the only one who would wish to say that if anybody has been captivated by a figment it is Mr Allegro.

9

Although Christianity has been rejected and ridiculed a thousand ways, nobody before Mr Allegro had thought of suggesting that it all started with a misunderstanding about a red and white spotted mushroom. *The Sacred Mushroom and the Cross* had one great merit: novelty. It was novelty that gained for it a popular audience when many scholars dismissed it out of hand; it was novelty that made it interesting to Christians and non-Christians alike. But the novelty of Mr. Allegro's theory must not obscure the fact that the true significance of *The Sacred Mushroom and the Cross* lies in its being representative, representative not of the speculations of an eccentric philologist but of a sceptical attitude to the Christian faith. Mr Allegro's book is in fact significant because it is a milestone. An unusually flamboyant milestone it certainly is, but the significance of a milestone lies not in its shape and size but in what it represents, and Mr Allegro's milestone marks a stage in an increasing disenchantment with dogma, tradition and orthodoxy. To put the matter another way, Mr Allegro is notable not so much for his fugitive theory as for the representative position he occupies as a debunker and contemner of traditional Christian belief.

By writing *The Sacred Mushroom and the Cross* Mr Allegro has invited people at large to regard Christianity as nothing more than a perverted fertility cult and has invested this view with the trappings of academic respectability. Without doubt Mr Allegro has hitherto shown himself to be a man of academic ability; he also has an ingenious, subtle and powerful imagination. In *The Sacred Mushroom and the Cross* he has produced what many people will welcome, an assurance that Christianity is a bombastic sham that can safely be ignored by intelligent people today. "Never mind about the details," many people will say, "they have to be left to the experts, anyway. What is important to us is the fact that a university teacher who is an acknowledged authority on such recent developments as the

10

Dead Sea Scrolls believes this, so there must be something in it." Regrettable as this attitude may be, it must be reckoned with. When a respected academic airs a theory that makes Christianity look totally ridiculous, he is making it that much easier for everybody to dismiss Christianity. Who can blame a non-reader for choosing not to believe the Christian Gospel after hearing a second-hand version of its origins according to Mr Allegro?

As far as his fellow academics are concerned, Mr Allegro's mushroom can be allowed to stew in its own juice; it is unlikely to cause many sleepless nights in the theological faculties. But in view of the publicity given to the theory at a popular level, in view of prevailing indifference to Christian dogma, in view of a hazy popular notion that the mushroom has proved to be yet another nail in the coffin of Christian belief, it needs to be said that men of common sense and Christian faith are still passionately committed to the Gospel of Jesus Christ, that a reading of the New Testament in the light of Mr Allegro's proposals makes the Gospel seem more, not less, convincing, that the figure of Jesus Christ the Son of God appears more, not less, commanding, and that far from demolishing Christian belief Mr Allegro has made its proportions and depth so freshly astounding that the poor little mushroom from under the pine trees seems, by comparison, to float aimlessly into nowhere like a scrap of paper released from a space capsule. A thoughtful reading of Mr Allegro's book serves, in fact, to remind the Christian reader of the greatness of the Gospel and of the inadequacy of man's inventive powers beside the utterances of the one who spake with authority and not as the scribes.

Mr Allegro's reading of the New Testament is a travesty, a grotesque and immoderate travesty, but it is a plausible travesty because it proposes a novel and fundamental re-interpretation of familiar patterns of thought. It has the plausibility that one finds in astute politicians who are able to turn electoral set-

11

backs, depressing public opinion polls and a poor record to their own advantage by means of a bold front and a measure of ingenuity. Mr Allegro's theory also gains plausibility by virtue of its sexual aspect. A generation that deliberates solemnly upon any question related to sexual behaviour will hardly dismiss out of hand a specious theory that shows the Christian faith to be a camouflaged sex-drama. Convincing or not in the light of a fresh reading of the New Testament, the mushroom theory cannot but gain currency and create an impression that Christianity has been caught with its slip showing, that Christians have a gigantic skeleton in the cupboard, that religious leaders have been the victims of a colossal confidence trick, that stripped of its finery and trappings the Christian religion is no more than a degenerate form of a stylised sex-game. We orthodox Christians have only ourselves to blame if we ignore the whole thing and allow the idea to gain acceptance that Christianity has had its day.

In all its juicy details and in all its speculative ramifications, then, the mushroom theory deserves at least a sharp repudiation. Scholars will doubtless argue learnedly over Sumerian verbal forms and the difference between Pliny's hellebore and Mr Allegro's fly agaric. We lesser mortals must make up our minds on the basis of common sense and an understanding of the general credibility and record of the Christian Gospel. Mr Allegro's book should be seen, in fact, as an opportunity of restating belief in full-blooded supernatural Christianity. While the mushroom remains at least a dim recollection, it can be made plain that many people today believe unequivocally that Jesus the Son of God performed miracles, died at the hands of the Romans, rose from the dead, ascended into heaven and one day will come again to judge the world. Here is one more invitation for us Christians to emerge from our religious clubs, to get off our home ground, to disengage our piety from the arum lilies, the coloured glass and the encaustic tiles, and to demonstrate that the Christian Gospel is credible, meaningful and compelling today. If Mr Allegro's book inspires us to tackle this task with new energy and imagination, if it inspires us to argue for the Gospel of Christ among the readers of *The Naked Ape* it will have achieved something – even if what it achieves is not exactly what its writer intended.

The sacred mush of May

"An hour after the ingestion of the mushrooms, twitching and trembling of the limbs is noticeable, with the onset of a period of good humour and light euphoria, characterised by macroscopia, visions of the supernatural and illusions of grandeur."

Quoted from R.E. Schultes by
John M. Allegro, *The Sacred Mushroom and the Cross*

When the summer months have included a general election, a cancelled South African cricket tour and the usual quota of strikes, storms and traffic jams, it may be necessary to make something of an effort to recall exactly how the sacred mushroom theory first came to public notice.

It was in February, 1970 that readers of the *Sunday Mirror* were first made aware that Erich von Daniken and his astronauts had now been superseded by John M. Allegro and his mushrooms. "Some will accuse me of blasphemy" said a headline underneath a front-page picture of Mr Allegro dutifully examining a dried specimen of the *amanita muscaria.* A fungus that mothers warn their children against had at last come into its own. In April more details were forthcoming. "Worship by orgy turned these women into witches" said the heading of a second extract from *The Sacred Mushroom and the Cross* published by the *Sunday Mirror* on April 19. A sub-heading explained: "A startling theory that Christianity is a hoax based on a sex-drug cult." Accompanying the extract was a striking illustration of Christ extended not against a cross but against a mushroom. The mushroom, sliced down the middle, hovered over a chequered board and shared the space with a sculptured female form of exaggerated proportions. But the sacred mushroom was not having things all its own way. Even in April, before a general election had been announced, other matters were competing for attention. An exclusive series by Sir Alf Ramsey on the inside story of the World Cup was beginning in the same issue, and the front page was almost entirely given over to an announcement about the series.

17

As far as its content was concerned, *The Sacred Mushroom and the Cross* should have been the ideal book to serialise in a newspaper whose readers like excitement. The book amounted to a devastating indictment of accepted religion and it had enough sex and drug-taking to make it supremely palatable. But when the sixty-three shilling volume was published on May 18 it became plain that the book itself, whatever its subject-matter, made few concessions to popular taste in the way of style. For all its extravagant speculation, the book appeared to have been designed as an academic production. Presentation was spare and dead-pan, even dull. Extensive re-writing had been necessary to make Mr Allegro's theory readable by *Sunday Mirror* readers. Anybody coming to the book from the serialisation would have found himself tackling a weighty assignment – not least the scholarly apparatus, notes and indices (but no bibliography), which he would have bumped into half-way through the book. Unless he was acquainted with the Sumerian, Accadian, Syriac, Greek and other systems of writing, he would have retired baffled.

"Who is this John Allegro?" such a reader might have been tempted to ask. The answer had already been given in the *Sunday Mirror* of April 12. Above the words "Next Sunday – the role of women in the sacred cults" was the unassuming countenance of a mild-mannered man who was already famous as the author of a well-known Pelican paperback, *The Dead Sea Scrolls. Who's Who* listed the impressive achievements of this 42-year-old ex-university lecturer – his academic awards, his leadership of archaeological expeditions to Jordan, the titles of his books. One of the books proves illuminating to the reader; it is *The Shapira Affair.* This serves not only to demonstrate, by contrast, the academic intention behind *The Sacred Mushroom and the Cross* for it indicates quite clearly that Mr Allegro has another style at his disposal, a line of colourful, swinging narrative that carries the reader along briskly and happily.

The Shapira Affair also has a theme which must have given Mr Allegro a good deal of food for thought, for it concerns the story of a little Slavonic Jew named Moses Shapira who claimed to have found in the vicinity of the Dead Sea an early version of Deuteronomy. The book recounts Shapira's unhappy collision with established scholars and a succession of frustrations that ended in his committing suicide in Rotterdam. The book reveals Mr Allegro's sympathy for Shapira in his solitary stand and Mr Allegro's slight regard for the "nineteenth century pundits" who declined to give an unprejudiced hearing to a discovery that might have proved inconvenient to the world of scholarship.

When *The Sacred Mushroom and the Cross* was published, it was received sceptically by reviewers. So specialised was the philological foundation on which Mr Allegro had built his case that competent critics who could deal adequately with the book at a scholarly level and produce at least a preliminary assessment of its likely importance were hard to find. Those reviewers who did discuss the book tended to leave Sumerian philology on one side and concentrate on weaknesses that were manifest to intelligent non-experts. The *Sunday Times* reviewer, a Jesuit by the name of Peter Levi, wrote: "The crucial arguments of Mr Allegro's attempt to establish the empire of fly-agaric over Judaism and Christianity are about the root meanings of words. I am not a professional philologist, and while he cross-breeds the consonants of Sumerian and Semitic languages I can only mumble dubiously that everyone knows you can prove anything you like by playing with word-roots. Nor is it of more than historical interest what the root of a word, say the name of a god, may be, if the people using that name can be shown to have been utterly unconscious of the sense of the philological root to which a modern scholar can attach it." But the Rev. Peter Levi then went on to discuss Mr Allegro's competence in the field of Greek (Fr Levi's own

19

subject) and wrote: "... Mr Allegro sometimes talks about Greek, and about this he talks such nonsense that it seems to me unsafe to take him seriously even as a philologist." Mr Levi's view was that Mr Allegro "is hardly to be taken seriously on his own ground, and not at all when he leaves it. He appears to be obsessed with a subject which has wasted years of his talents."

In the *Observer* Joel Carmichael was less peremptory in his dismissal of Mr Allegro's book as a serious contribution to scholarship but his verdict was similar. Mr Allegro, he said, had resorted to "the circular reasoning that is so often the refuge of daring innovators." Mr Carmichael went on: "I hope I am not being unfair to Mr Allegro when I say that his book strikes me as rather 'trendy'. Not merely does the whole idea of the book revolve around drug-taking − a fashionable contemporary obsession − but Mr Allegro lays a curiously heavy emphasis on sexuality, still more fashionable." Mr Carmichael acknowledged in his review the shortage of specialists in the field which Mr Allegro had so diligently cultivated: "Mr Allegro's book is studded with references to philological affinities between Biblical Hebrew, Aramaic, Arabic, Greek and especially Sumerian (which few have a working knowledge of)." Mr Carmichael confined himself, like other reviewers, to the improbabilities inherent in the structure erected by Mr Allegro on his philological foundation.

The Dean of Christ Church, Oxford, Dr Henry Chadwick, was notably forthright. In the *Daily Telegraph* of May 21 he wrote: "Mr Allegro's reputation as a man of judgment and learning, already widely questioned, is likely to be shattered by this curious publication. His new book reads like a Semitic philologist's erotic nightmare after consuming a highly indigestible meal of hallucinogenic fungi." Dr Chadwick referred to Mr Allegro's "bizarre hypothesis", to "rich indulgence in the wildest flights of uncontrolled fantasy", to "uncanny decipherment" and to a "luxuriant farrago of nonsense". In conclusion

Dr Chadwick wrote: "Perhaps there may be some sad minds to whom his book offers a liberating experience. But three guineas' worth of *Amanita muscaria* would be better value." Dr Chadwick allowed himself a certain amount of irony at Mr Allegro's expense, but not so much as Nigel Dennis had allowed himself in the *Sunday Telegraph* a few days before: Mr Dennis asked why readers of Mr Allegro's book should allow themselves to be converted by one "whose arguments are really a disgrace to the proud Manchester school of rationalism? We cannot argue *back*, of course, because there cannot be any argument with a man who argues that there's no evidence like no evidence. We can only wish him and his Amanita (what a charming name for a girl, by the way) a happy fruitful relationship." Referring to the appendices, Mr Dennis concluded: "As only some half-dozen English scholars are equipped to take a bash at these, the rest of us can only hope that the professor has not strained his learning as much as he has strained his ignorance."

In the *Guardian* of May 21 Professor Ninian Smart expressed doubt whether Mr Allegro's latest hypothesis would lead to confidence in his inferences and judgments. "The book doubtless will sell well. It leads me to poetic nostalgia," he wrote, and concluded his review with some verse:

Though the Church at the start was quite smart, she
Got distorted and solemn and starchy.
Phallic mushrooms are gone
And the Pope's not switched on,
When he *could* be *allegro vivace.*

Dennis Potter, in *The Times Saturday Review* of May 23, wrote entertainingly of Mr Allegro's ability as a philologist to explain "the history of a word without having the slightest inkling of the ways in which language itself works." But he, like others, was forced to write around the book rather than to venture into the fields of mycology and philology where Mr Allegro had actually been at work. Mr Potter did state one impression made by Mr Allegro's book. Mr Allegro appeared to him to be "a scholarly, perceptive, quirkily talented man who somewhere along the way—and while immersed in the language and the teeming quarries of faith—has developed an intense antipathy to the whole great edifice of Christianity." Mr Potter also said: "the full thrust of the thesis is directed head on against the figure of Christ."

Meanwhile, back at the *Sunday Mirror*, Mr Allegro was getting summary treatment. In an article published on May 17 under the heading "A load of old fungus!" the Rev Michael Green, Principal of the London College of Divinity, dismissed the book. He accused Mr Allegro of being infatuated with sex, of having a highly suspect judgment, of having a bizarre under-standing of pagan religions, and of showing anti-Christian prejudice. An editorial note at the top of the page "Last word on the Sacred Mushroom" suggested that readers had had enough of mushrooms. On another page Mrs Gladys Packer of Cheltenham had the following letter published: "So the beautiful fairy tale of Snow White is to be desecrated by the film producers and the innocent dwarfs turned into sadists." There will not be anything sacred or beautiful left presently." One might almost conclude that by allowing his book to be serialised for the benefit of readers agog for revelations from eccentric aristocrats, retired detectives and football chiefs Mr Allegro was playing in the wrong league.

It was Robert Graves who, in the *New Statesman* of May 15, gave certain aspects of Mr Allegro's theory most serious atten-tion. Mr Graves was in a stronger position than many because he had already taken an interest in the *amanita muscaria* – to such an extent that he had described its connection with Dionysus in *Food for Centaurs*. Mr Graves was also in the position of having in his garden in Majorca a paeony of the kind described by Pliny, not the shrubby perennial with big blooms that we see in our gardens but a plant that grows on shaded mountains and bears four or five growths like almonds. Mr Graves detected in Mr Allegro "a growing revulsion against the rigorous nonconformity in which he was brought up" and considered that this had tempted him to publish "a thoroughly off-beat book". Mr Graves went on to chide Mr Allegro with his lack of botanical knowledge and to ask how supplies of the mushroom could have been made available to members of the mushroom sect in Judaea. Another blind spot pointed out by Mr Graves was Mr Allegro's failure to refer to the pine as a host tree, but on Mr Allegro's behalf it must be pointed out that in a note on page 292 he does refer to the mushroom being found in coniferous forests. Mr Graves described the occasion on which he tasted manna at the invitation of the President of Israel but disclaimed any experience of having tasted the fly agaric. Friends of his, however, who had tasted the fungus had told him that the fly agaric tasted very much like any other mushroom, especially if one peeled it. But here Mr Allegro may well say that the bitter, burning taste to which he refers is indeed found under the rind (page 152).

In the religious press most reviewers laboured to be fair but found Mr Allegro's theory light-weight and unconvincing. Canon Max Warren, who reviewed the book for the *Church Times,* was not the only one to ask: "Is John Allegro's new book a hoax?" Canon Warren wrote: "An investigator of the origins of Christianity who can seriously argue that the writers of the four Gospels were in league to invent a story as a cover for taking drugs; who can be so insensitive to aesthetic values as to picture a cryptographer producing I Corinthians 13, presumably as providing initiates with erotic entertainment; who can imagine that the argument of Galatians or Romans is not really concerned with law, sin and grace but represents the meanderings of the mind of a man called Paul who, under the mystic influence of the mushroom drug, experienced one of those flashes of light which are said to be characteristic products of chewing the fungus, and so provides an explanation of that non-event on the Damascus Road; that, in a word, the New Testament is an elaborate lie — any investigator who comes up with these conclusions can hardly be expected to be taken seriously."

In a leading article the *Church Times* expressed confidence in the ability of scholars to deal with "this fantastic book" but said that the book needed attention for two reasons: the academic standing of Mr Allegro and the widespread publicity given to the mushroom theory by pre-publication serialisation in a popular Sunday newspaper. The leading article asserted the actuality of the events upon which the Christian faith is based. "And the meaning and power of those events have been proved in countless converted lives . . ."

In the *Catholic Herald* Dom Sylvester Houedard fastened on the philology as the vital issue. "But what, in fact, is the truth in all this?" he asked, and went on to say, "Possibly quite a lot, at least round the edge of the theory; it is the centre that's rather thin. To know if Sumerian is the bridge between the Indo-European and the Semitic languages spade work has to be done by etymologists." Another point emphasised by the *Catholic Herald* reviewer was the high proportion of speculative Sumerian verbal forms appearing in Mr Allegro's book. "The Sumerian index contains, at a rough count, 875 entries of which 404 are provided with asterisks; to me this seems far too high a percentage to justify the confidence of a great many assertions . . ."

Reviewing the book in the *Baptist Times*, Noel Schofield made his introductory sentence: "This is the most fantastic and misleading book I have ever been asked to review."

Mr Allegro had fallen between two stools. By appealing to the general public over the heads of fellow-scholars he had alienated possible philological sympathisers. Conscientious philologists were affronted to find extravagantly elaborated theories being discussed when a meticulous investigation of philological findings was required. Instead of a closely argued contest over Sumerian texts there took place a short-lived fire-work display in connection with remote and fanciful deductions. Instead of learned debate there were brief references on the radio for the benefit of commuters rushing through their breakfasts and weekenders sitting down to their roast beef. Mr Allegro was introducing a speculative explanation of the origins of Christianity that rested upon untested philological research conducted by himself. Only criticism of his basic research by expert philologists could establish whether he was entitled to go on to build a theory and offer it to the public. In the eyes of fellow scholars, then, Mr Allegro was both extravagant and premature.

Mr Allegro's chances of being taken seriously by fellow scholars suffered a severe blow when on May 26 *The Times* published a letter from Professor Sir Godfrey Driver of Oxford and fourteen other scholars. In it they state their view that the book is not based on any philological or other evidence which they could regard as scholarly. Among the signatories were professors of Semitic languages and Hebrew at the universities of Cambridge, London and Manchester.

The letter can scarcely have come as a surprise to Mr Allegro. In 1956 he had been similarly dismissed by fellow scholars writing to *The Times* to dissociate themselves from his interpretation of the Dead Sea Scrolls. This, however, had not prevented his book *The Dead Sea Scrolls* from selling a quarter of a million copies. His reputation probably suffered little as a result of appearing to be a man of original and independent mind at odds with the academic establishment.

In the course of writing this book I was in touch with a number of scholars, philologists and others. They were all

25

exceedingly helpful and generous in giving me their time, but despite their patient and kindly manner there was no disguising the fact that they had dismissed *The Sacred Mushroom and the Cross* as not worthy of any serious notice. In their view the book was fanciful. Mr Allegro had rushed into a little-understood linguistic field where no self-respecting angel would ever dare to tread. I was told that Mr Allegro's book was an offence not against religion but against reason, that there was no particle of historical evidence for a mushroom religion, that he made assertions impossible to prove. One eminent scholar told me that he had never seen a mushroom in Palestine; another regretted the absence of references in the book to learned discussion of the matters under consideration. Such were the comments on the unsatisfactory nature of Mr Allegro's philological methods, on his fantasy, on his ignorance of botany that the inquirer was forced to conclude that someone, somewhere along the line, had made a great error of judgment in allowing the theory to see the light of day. Increasingly Mr Allegro took on the appearance of either a misguided enthusiast dealing with matters outside his competence or a heroic seeker after truth persisting in fidelity to his convictions despite the serried ranks of orthodox scholars. There were even those who mentioned the possibility that Mr Allegro was indulging in a leg-pull. It is not unknown, of course, for one scholar to be right and for all the rest to be wrong, but it must be said that if Mr Allegro ever does succeed in persuading fellow academics to reverse their judgments about his theory he will have achieved something even more difficult than persuading Conservatives to elect Mr Harold Wilson to leadership of the Conservative Party. Scholars will just not take Mr Allegro and his book seriously.

At the popular level it was indubitably noticed. Professor Ninian Smart quoted one reader of the *Sunday Mirror* as saying: "I always believed that the Bible was a lot of rubbish:

now I know it—this Allegro is a well-known scholar." On May 28 the London *Evening News* put the book fourth in its top ten. Mr Allegro's book did not, however, have the impact it might have had if he had written it in the style he had employed for *The Shapira Affair*. It was the extracts in the *Sunday Mirror*, rewritten extracts, that had ensured *The Sacred Mushroom and the Cross* a place in the bookshops alongside Erich von Daniken's best-seller, *Chariots of the Gods?* Mr Allegro's book had been written in colourless academic prose, with what C. S. Lewis used to call the unlaid ghost of a *sententia* beginning a chapter as often as not; there was none of the brisk, punchy, "gods from outer space" stuff that had sold over 400,000 copies of von Daniken's book in Germany. For twenty-four hours the mushroom commanded popular attention; then the news of a forthcoming general election and the row over the South African cricket tour gave people other things to think about. At the end of it all there were a handful of scholars looking quizzically at Mr Allegro's footnotes, a few thousand people who had put down their names for the book at the nearest public library, and a mass of people who had collected vague notions that God, who had recently been shown to be an astronaut from elsewhere in the universe, had now been shown to be nothing more than a mushroom worshipped by a drug-mad fertility cult. Scholars smiled; many people giggled; a number thought there must be *something* in it.

It must of course be acknowledged that as I write, *The Sacred Mushroom and the Cross* has not been published in America, or in its foreign translations and there is no way of telling how scholars and reviewers outside Britain will react.

Philologist's breakthrough?

Now we face a new revolution in thought which must make us reconsider the validity of the New Testament story. The break-through here is not in the field of history but in philology.

John M. Allegro, *The Sacred Mushroom and the Cross*

The day before *The Sacred Mushroom and the Cross* was published, I happened to be preaching in a school chapel. Immediately after the service I was talking to the school chaplain and his family. Horse-chestnuts were in blossom by the cricket-pitch and a flag was hanging limply on the flag-pole. The English Sunday morning had reached the flat spot between the morning service and The World this Weekend. All was traditional and secure – almost to the point of caricature. I happened to ask the chaplain's little son what he had been reading while I was preaching. He showed me his picture-book. Imagine my surprise when I saw on the stiff cover a colourful representation of what looked uncommonly like the fly agaric. On an inside page was another specimen, this one being eyed by a cheerful-looking toad ensconced on a made-to-measure toadstool. Peace, tradition and security were shattered by the appearance of this gaily coloured mushroom, for here in the hands of an uncomprehending child was the secret of the ages, the ultimate symbol of sex and religion, a symbol more primitive, more powerful, more meaningful than the cross of Christ. At least, Mr Allegro would have us believe that the fungus has this kind of importance.

The next day the general election was announced and Mr Allegro's mushroom disappeared from view under a welter of opinion poll reports and political comment. But for some people the clue had been there all the time. They are the people whose doctors are thoughtful enough to provide in their

31

waiting-rooms not only old copies of the *Illustrated London News* and *Vogue* but also the posters supplied by the Royal Society for the Prevention of Accidents about dangerous berries and poisonous fungi. There in the bottom left-hand corner of the fungi poster was the red and white topped mushroom, one mushroom amongst many, but a mushroom, as Mr Allegro was to reveal, of immense significance to any man taking the New Testament seriously.

In Mr Allegro's hands the mushroom serves as a symbol of the crass gullibility of generations of Christians. He debunks Christianity and he debunks it thoroughly. He does not merely argue that it is untrue and damaging, as Lord Russell used to do; Mr Allegro argues that it is perverted. Christianity, he says, is nothing more than a misguided offshoot of an ancient fertility rite; in all probability Jesus never existed; the very names we use for God are nothing more than misappropriated sexual terms; the Ten Commandments and the Lord's Prayer are no more than drug-takers' recruitment literature; the Old Testament is an enigmatic compendium of assorted religious views of varying merit; the New Testament is a hoax which has been unexpectedly honoured by men who have taken it seriously. Mr Allegro's discoveries about the mushroom gave Christianity the appearance of a discreditable farce. At last the Christian faith was exposed for the miserable thing it was. The idea was simple enough; if you strip away the pomp and tradition, all that you have left is the kind of mushroom that is found in children's picture-books.

Since Mr Allegro reduces all Christians to the same level, a level at which we miserably clutch a colourful mushroom under the delusion that we are clinging to Almighty God, a God who has supremely spoken and acted and revealed himself in Jesus Christ, we do well to place this particular theory in its historical perspective. In century after century the Church has been intimidated by tyrants, denigrated by opponents, mutilated by politicians, enervated by seductive governments, torn asunder by the squabbles of reactionaries and reformers, and made a laughing-stock by some of its most enthusiastic supporters. Mr Allegro is not the first to set himself the task of toppling the Church and it is unlikely that he will be the last. In the midst of the confusion and conflict there has always been a succession of men and women whose shining faith and loyalty to Christ have triumphed over onslaught from outside and mutiny from within. To counter-balance the Borgias, the Inquisition and the Erastians there has been a St Francis or a Father Damien or a John Wesley. Theories about astronauts and mushrooms are assaults by pea-shooter compared with the projectiles from siege-artillery and the uprisings in the citadel that have shaken the Church in one generation after another. The survival power of the Gospel and of the Church has to be remembered whenever a new assault is mounted or a new mutiny breaks out.

The idea that Christianity is based on nothing more substantial than a mushroom has to be seen then against the background of numerous other essays in debunking and despoiling the Church. We have been this way before. But the angle of attack on this occasion has to be noted. In the case presented by Mr Allegro the mushroom is the achievement and the colourful symbol of success, not the point of departure. It might be thought that it is an interest in botany that led Mr Allegro to his startling conclusions. But this is not the case. The botanical evidence is dubious and incidental; its function is to confirm a view already held on other grounds. Mr Allegro's case is developed from a philological basis. Taking as his point of departure the notion that Sumerian is a common source of the Indo-European and Semitic groups of languages, he finds innumerable mushroom references in the vocabulary of the Old and New Testaments. As he himself insists, it is words and ideas rather than history and people that form the starting-point for his theory.

Mr Allegro has mounted an assault on the philological front. He does not cast himself in the role of an Amalekite harrying the Chosen People; nor does he see himself as a Philistine stretching out a temerarious hand to touch the Ark of the Covenant. He is simply a philologist going about his philological duties and, in the process, uncovering some novel information about the vocabulary of the Bible. (Perhaps he will be prepared, on reflection, to concede that he is a little more than a philologist, for he has allowed himself to venture into the field of botany and he has also allowed himself to build an extremely weighty and speculative structure upon his philological findings; but that his main thrust is philological cannot be doubted.) Mr Allegro not only performed what he regards as his philological duty; he has also contrived to show himself an extremely adept public relations officer in the service of philology. Those who had never heard of the subject, or had imagined philologists to be palely preoccupied with Grimm's Law, vowel-shifts, crumbling old documents and the phonetics of everyday conversation will have to think again. Mr Allegro has demonstrated —to his own satisfaction, at least — that philology is a weapon mighty to the pulling down of strongholds, even the stronghold that we call Christianity. Obviously very few people will now be rushing out to order a Sumerian grammar or an anthology of Sumerian texts; but many will have registered the point that philology can upset archbishops and make a hash of Christian belief. There will be a new popular respect for the man who traces the history of language; philology, it will be realised, is not merely a dusty hobby for withered old men with beards and bi-focals; it is an exceedingly powerful tool that can overturn conventional religious thought. By opening his word-hoard and putting on show his latest specimens of ancient — and modern — polysyllables from the Persian Gulf, Mr Allegro has opened a new, philological, front between Christians and their opponents.

Where Christians and non-Christians once argued over Cain's wife, they will now dispute the significance of Sumerian compounds. In order to survive we Christians, or some of our representatives, will have to apply ourselves to philology.

Consider Mr Allegro at work. Former generations would have dubbed him a heresiarch. We in our generation do not require our researchers to come to orthodox Christian conclusions. Mr Allegro accordingly wears the blameless mantle of a philologist and his philology has also led him to be an amateur of wild flowers and fungi. Patiently he excavates around the base of the Christian Church, descends into the trial diggings, declares that the so-called foundations are no more than phallic symbols and alkaloids, and waits for the whole structure to collapse before his eyes. As a result of his philological inquiry he labels the enduring edifice of the Christian Church, surviving through generations of persecution, neglect and mockery, as a pretentious structure based on a ludicrous misunderstanding. Like Euston arch, said to have been built on a scale ten times that envisaged by its designer because of the ineptitude of some underling, the Church is said to have been erected by well-intentioned simpletons who were unaware of the original purpose of the designers. What should have been no more than a pleasing façade has been turned into a commodious complex. Mr Allegro, however, has directed our attention to the misunderstanding. With the philological equivalent of pick and shovel he has exposed enough of the foundations for others to carry on the revealing work. It is only a matter of time before sufficient people have carried on where Mr Allegro left off to make it impossible for the building to stand any longer. After all, phallic symbols and alkaloids provide adequate foundations only so long as they are unseen and unsuspected. When they have been patiently and incontrovertibly revealed to the public gaze, the building on which they stand will inevitably collapse. After the crash,

35

says Mr Allegro, we can construct some more reasonable ethical framework on which to shape our individual lives and our society.

Philology could have no better demonstration of its effectiveness than this. Implicit in every line of Mr Allegro's book is the spectacular consequence of following out his thought to its conclusion. The Christian Church will crash to confusion because a single-minded philologist had the independence of mind to trace Greek and Hebrew words back to their Sumerian originals. And this he achieved in the face of colleagues' scepticism. When other philologists doubted, one amongst them had the faith to persevere.

To be confronted with philology coming into its own in this way is like seeing Grandma come downstairs in a mini-skirt and hair-piece declaring her intention of painting the town red. It is obvious to all that after such a display the existence of Grandma cannot possibly be ignored; but mingled with appreciation of the impact made by such an unpredicted move is a certain amount of apprehension about her reputation. None the less, whatever else he may have done, Mr Allegro has given a new look to philology. He has taken a hitherto severely academic subject out of the academic cloisters and demonstrated its power. If philology from now on is ever regarded as an arid study, suitable only for "Bald heads, forgetful of their sins", it will not be Mr Allegro's fault. He has given philology a chance to prove itself in popular estimation by no less a feat than the demolition of Christianity. What has proved too great a task for dictators, philosophers and unsympathetic theologians is to be made a philological contest. The palm for achieving the overthrow of orthodox Christianity is to be reserved for a lover of words, a phoneme-sifter. At least – the palm will be awarded *if* Mr Allegro can convince his readers. If not, he will have to accept the consolation prize of knowing that he has stimulated popular interest in philology; and the knowledge that he has made men uneasy about barbarous neologisms and helped them to be more discriminating about the words they daily squander and abuse must be no small consolation to any philologist in this word-weary and meretricious age.

No philologist will expect to make friends among the Christians by announcing discoveries such as these. After all, nobody likes to come home at the end of the day to find a stranger assiduously digging out the foundations from under his house, and no man can claim to have exposed as fraudulent the most sacred elements in any religion without incurring some obloquy. Mr Allegro will expect rejoinders. He will also, I am afraid, expect shrill charges about opening the flood-gates of blasphemy, and probably of obscenity too. We Christians have no reason to be so fearful of our standing that we must scream at any man who dares to question our beliefs. Nor should we have any reason for shunning explicit discussion of sexual matters when the argument requires it. If Mr Allegro is honestly persuaded in the face of numerous colossal improbabilities that Christianity is based on nothing more than a mushroom, he is perfectly entitled to his opinion. "I disapprove of what you say, but I will defend to the death your right to say it" is a proper sentiment for a Christian to voice.

Mr Allegro makes it plain that the kind of breakthrough he believes himself to have accomplished is the demonstration of a linguistic bridge between the Indo-European and Semitic languages. In Sumerian he finds "a common, recoverable source" from which Greek and Hebrew — to name specific members of the two linguistic families — are derived. By accepting the basic Sumerian vocabulary, subsequent neighbouring cultures necessarily took over the underlying philosophical attitudes of the early Sumerians. This linguistic point is by no means conceded by Mr Allegro's fellow scholars (indeed, it is rejected), but it is this point which he elaborates from specific words throughout his book, and it is on the

37

validity of this point that the value of the entire book depends.

Other people will judge that Mr Allegro has made a break-through of quite a different kind; in *The Sacred Mushroom and the Cross* he has succeeded in reaching a popular audience with novel theological ideas. He has achieved this popular impact by propounding a startling theory about a mushroom. The theory is pictorial rather than conceptual; it is uncompli-cated by traditional dogmatic language (no bothering with words like "incarnation" and "kenosis"); it appears to offer a simple explanation of matters that theologians have monopol-ised and made incomprehensible. However much eminent scholars may question Mr Allegro, the matter has moved out of their territory and has made an appeal to the popular imagina-tion. Once a theory such as this has established itself by a powerful appeal to the imagination, it cannot be ejected by austere academic argument alone; it becomes part of the folk-consciousness. It is like inventing a bull-dog or lion symbol to represent one's own nation; once the term is invented and is in currency, it shapes the way in which people think and feel about their fatherland; rational argument is relatively feeble to affect subsequent attitudes.

The fact, therefore, that philologists and others believe Mr Allegro's linguistic reasoning to be inadequate will not be sufficient to squash the mushroom theory. Mr Allegro has created a powerful symbol (originally, of course, on his terms it was more than a symbol), has justified its existence by ingenious word-play and has been enabled to present it favoura-bly to a receptive readership. Whatever scholars may say about the linguistic points which Mr Allegro introduces in connection with his assertions will scarcely affect the mushroom idea itself. What matters in Mr Allegro's book is the positive symbol. The philological case upon which the symbol must be based is presented in passing; it is not seriously argued. The all-important matter is the mushroom. When the philologists have finished with Mr Allegro's supposed breakthrough, the mush-room will remain.

Because a man puts philology on the map by presenting his findings in such a way as to discredit the traditional under-standing of the Christian faith, he must not necessarily be accused of hawking his wares in a strident and unbecoming manner. It would certainly be inappropriate for us Christians to complain that heretics or unbelievers, whether aided by *Sunday Mirror* sub-editors or not, are able to capture the popu-lar imagination, while we merely sit by and wring our hands. As the former Bishop of Woolwich has said, there is much work to be done on the frontier between theology and journal-ism. If Mr Allegro is not setting out to do that work in the service of the Gospel, he is at least opening the way for others to do so. The most innocent reader of newspapers knows that a headline "Babies by proxy" is likely to ensure a readership a hundred times greater than a sober treatment of some new development in implanting fertilised ova in the wombs of other women. A matter that is entirely overlooked by the public if it is presented in terms of serious objectivity will set the Thames on fire if it is presented in terms of immediate personal applica-tion. We Christians must resist the temptation to complain that only the unorthodox get read; we must ourselves set out to be colourful and quotable; we for our part must, in the inter-ests of the Gospel, learn to catch the popular imagination.

Not the least of the lessons to be learned from the impact made by Mr Allegro's book is the fact that we Christians are far from adept at gaining the popular ear. We owe it to the Gospel to give far more thought to the question of presentation and interpretation. All too often it is we who imprison the Gospel within dull words, clichés and tired anecdotes. We must not fail to give Mr Allegro credit for an active imagination and we must stir up our own imaginations to make the kind of breakthrough that he has made. If we should shrink from this

39

kind of activity, if we should say that we are unwilling to make ourselves as culpable as Mr Allegro in presenting sensational material to undiscriminating readers, we have to consider what kind of popular impact we are having at present. Do the books that are most successful on our church bookstalls succeed in popularising the Gospel without trivialising it? Is our popular literature genuinely popular? Nothing is easier than for us Christians to deceive ourselves about whether we have made a breakthrough, Allegro-style to vast numbers of people.

To those who have regarded the Bible as a book of immense dignity, properly embalmed in seventeenth century English of unvarying majesty and utterly remote from the commonplace concerns of life, let alone such subjects as copulation, impregnation and menstruation that are best not mentioned at all and certainly not in connection with religion, Mr Allegro's findings will come as a shock. The Bible is an elevating book, it may be felt, and to take it from the lectern and worry out its meaning in popular, everyday, earthy terms is quite improper and probably indecent. It must be remembered, however, that there is much in the Bible that cannot decently be read in public (at least, not in a version that the hearers will understand) and that it is only the fact that we rarely read the Bible completely through that prevents us from noticing the abundance of material dealing with prohibited sexual activity and ceremonial requirements of a sexual nature. Some of this material is necessarily dealt with in any discussion of the possible origin of Christianity in early fertility religion. The Bible is not a prudish book, and the man who is taking it seriously – whatever his views – cannot afford to be prudish himself.

I ask the reader's indulgence if the matters dealt with in the following pages seem to be indecent. Mr Allegro has dealt explicitly with a range of sexual matters, and so must anybody who considers the points he makes. When a scholar tells us that the Bible is little more than a camouflaged guide for fertility-worshippers, we cannot bury our heads in the sand and pretend that nothing has happened. We have to understand the charges and make a response. This being so, one cannot discuss Mr Allegro's case without mentioning the unmentionable, and the charge of indecency is easily incurred in this field. Let the reader be warned that much of what follows is for adult readers.

It is not enough to reproach Mr Allegro for doing philological research and expressing the results in popular terms, neither is it enough to dismiss his ubiquitous phallic imagery and to opt for a world from which phallic imagery has been banned. The mushroom is going to rear its symbolic head in every R.E. lesson and every club-room discussion. The basic idea is clear enough for everybody to grasp and Christians everywhere are going to find themselves defensively falling back as they are pressed on to unfamiliar ground by sceptical fungus-wielders. What can Christians say when they are accused of clinging to doctrines whose hollowness has been exposed? Is it henceforth going to be possible for a Christian to say that he believes in the Son of God who died and rose again for his sins? Must a Christian turn abjectly and flee before every critic who flourishes a mushroom in his face? It is to these questions that we must address ourselves now.

41

Drug-takers' message

Here, then, was the literary device to spread occult knowledge to the faithful. To tell the story of a rabbi called Jesus, and invest him with the power and names of the magic drug.

John M. Allegro, *The Sacred Mushroom and the Cross*

What, briefly, has Mr Allegro put before his readers in *The Sacred Mushroom and the Cross*? He has provided a popular incentive to the study of philology and at a more serious level he has brought to light linguistic correspondences which may possibly be of value to those who make a study of the Semitic and other ancient languages. He has shed new light on ancient fertility religion and he has dismissed Christianity as a mere stalking-horse sheltering followers of a persecuted fertility cult. In a sentence, Mr Allegro has proposed that the New Testament was never meant to be read in a straightforward manner and has a hidden meaning which has only been revealed as a result of advances in philological research. Is the New Testament indeed a book with a hidden meaning? This is the prime question facing readers of Mr Allegro's book and it is a question which cannot be ignored. It is as though generations had happily read a defective copy of Spenser's *Faerie Queene* without being conscious of the allegorical significance and had been told that Spenser's introduction and give-away quatrains had been discovered. It is as though generations had happily read Swift's *Gulliver's Travels* (suitably expurgated) as a delightful nursery tale and had suddenly been informed that under cover of the story Swift was trying to say something about mankind. Mr Allegro is telling us that the generations that have happily read the New Testament as a story of the life, death and resurrection of the God-man have missed the point. But now blind eyes can be opened and the message can be read in clear for the first time.

45

It should not be thought, however, that Mr Allegro has provided a key to the interpretation of the New Testament — or more properly the whole Bible — which will now enable us to see a grand design, something like Spenser's grand design for *The Faerie Queene,* making itself plain in every one of the sixty-six books which make up the Old and New Testaments. Mr Allegro has not set himself such a stiff task, and indeed the nature of his proposal denies the possibility of demonstrating such a grand design. Mr Allegro has restricted himself to pointing out that here and there in the Bible are references to other, weightier matters than seem at first sight to be the things which preoccupy the biblical writers. Mr Allegro's case is not that the Bible is a beautifully executed allegory, the significance and unity of whose theme we can now appreciate for the first time. He is instead concerned to show that in a random collection of documents illustrating the hotch-potch of confusion and warring elements which we call Judaism and its off-shoot Christianity, there are hints and allusions pointing the reader to controversial and sometimes underground fertility cults which permeated the ancient world and determined the form taken by ancient religion.

We can now see, says Mr Allegro, that far from being revelations made by the Most High God, Judaism and Christianity are cultic expressions of man's search to discover the secrets at the heart of the universe. The "extra-terrestrial intelligence" that ensures the continuance of vegetable and animal life was obviously an important field of primeval human inquiry. Survival depended upon fitting in with his or its plans. The man who failed to discover the most effective way of stimulating crop-growth and animal-breeding would find himself without the resources to rise above his environment. He would fall never to rise again. Everything depended upon fertility. The frenzied quest for fertility must have been remarkably like the frenzied quest for telling ideas that characterises a present-day advertising agency. Just as the agency, to ensure its survival in a highly competitive field, must pray for an unfailing flow of ideas better than those of its rivals, so the primeval soil-scratcher and stock-rearer must have prayed for powerful seed that would enable yet another harvest to supply his needs. The zany antics adopted by advertising men summoning up ideas from the depths of their subconscious must make us diffident about dismissing the more formalised antics of the primitive farmers as nothing more than superstitious rigmarole.

By coupling in the open air on the fields which they hoped would prove fertile, the early farmers did their best to compensate for their ignorance of nitrates, phosphates and drainage. The farmer and his partner hoped that the forces of nature would take the hint and follow the humans' example. Later generations gradually learned wisdom. Whereas the older fertility cult followers sought to influence events, Jews and "Christians" (i.e. the fertility cult followers masquerading as Christians) came to restrict their activities to entering into the ultimate wisdom and predicting the future. The development is one that is paralleled by those who in the Middle Ages turned from magic to astrology. So it comes about, says Mr Allegro, that Judaism and Christianity are cultic expressions of man's search to discover God's secrets.

In general, followers of the fertility cults sought to attain what Christians have characteristically described as the vision of God. Instead, however, of resorting to prayer, the fertility worshippers turned to drugs. The only source of drugs available was the plants around them. Generations of sampling and observation (which must have involved a good many painful, not to say fatal, consequences) led the experimenters to confine their interest to the fungi and to one fungus in particular, the fly agaric, *amanita muscaria.* This member of the mushroom family, a plant which we should normally describe as a toadstool, contains a number of powerful drugs, one of which heightens perception. It was not only this, however, which earned it a high reputation; it displayed an elaborate sexual symbolism in the manner of its growth, its shape and its colour; it made its appearance mysteriously after rain (divine seed?) had impregnated the ground; both male and female genitals were thought to be symbolised in its component parts. It was bewitching, fascinating. Wherever it made its mysterious appearance it was a symbol of, and an incitement to, vigorous sexual performance. Those humans who were daring enough to move from contemplation to mastication found that it gave them the superhuman strength and ferocity later found in such widely separated groups as the zealots and berserkers. It was a plant to enable old men to see dreams and young men to see visions. It was indeed a prince among plants.

Knowledge of this plant and its properties was not something to be shouted abroad indiscriminately. Obviously here was a fungus to be treated with respect. Together with the awe appropriate to a plant in some way connected with the ruling power of the universe there was also in all probability a certain proprietary interest such as the alchemists, apothecaries and pharmaceutical manufacturers later displayed. Men are always jealous of their discoveries when they think that they and they alone have the secret. The guardians of the fly agaric therefore kept their information to themselves. When it was necessary to pass on advice about the recommended methods of gathering and swallowing the plant, this was done by word of mouth. Occasionally, however, the fertility worshippers would find themselves under unusual pressure from the authorities and they might then find it necessary to commit their secrets to writing. One such occasion was the time preceding the fall of Jerusalem in AD 70. As was customary, what was written down was put into a code for the sake of security. The result, says Mr Allegro, was the New Testament. Like their forebears who had tucked away information about properties and procedures to be borne in mind when dealing with the fly agaric, the fertility worshippers facing hostile authorities constructed a good cover. So effective was it that it has survived in its own right for nearly two thousand years. If they could have foreseen their work developing into an all-time best-seller, the literary servants of the fly agaric would doubtless have been more than a little surprised.

On this view Christianity is seen to be – when it is divested of its elaborations and accretions – a bizarre sideline to the onward march of fertility religion. So successful were the first century fertility worshippers in concealing their secrets by inventing the story of one Jesus that subsequent generations actually took the Jesus story seriously. They entirely lost track of the central feature of fertility religion, the consumption of fly agaric, and diligently elaborated the cover story so as to include (as Mr Allegro would have us believe) such grotesque parodies of the mushroom cult as the belief that the bread and wine of the Communion service are actually the body and blood of the Jesus of the cover story.

The New Testament is not, of course, the first literary composition to have an allegorical meaning extracted from, or read into it. We are all, for example, familiar with Augustine's view that the two pence that the good Samaritan paid to the innkeeper represent the two sacraments of the Gospel – Baptism and Holy Communion. We are probably familiar too with the mythological interpretations imposed upon the Old English heroic poem "Beowulf". Grendel and his mother, it has been said, symbolise the North Sea; Beowulf, who on this view is said to represent fruitfulness, checks the encroachments of the sea in the spring season. On another view Beowulf is regarded as a personification of wind and storm, and Grendel represents perhaps the long winter nights. Etymologists have suggested that the name of the hero of this eighth century poem meant "bee-wolf" or "enemy of the bees" (i.e. a woodpecker). Others

49

have considered that "bee-wolf" patently means a bear. It is also possible to read "Beowulf" as a piece of Christian symbolism in which Beowulf appears as a visitor on an errand of redemption who frees wretched men from bondage to the powers of darkness. It is possible to find an allegory, or the beginnings of an allegory, in this Old English poem, but it is presumptuous to be dogmatic about the matter. There are many imponderable factors in a poem of whose background we know so little; moderation and caution are appropriate.

Quite different is the best-known allegorical work in English, *Pilgrim's Progress.* Here the author's intention is plain; we read Bunyan's masterpiece as an allegory because the writer's purpose is signified in the title: "The Pilgrim's Progress from this world, to That which is to come: Delivered under the Similitude of a Dream Wherein is Discovered, The manner of his setting out, His Dangerous Journey; and safe Arrival at the Desired Countrey." We have only to recall that the poem which we call "Beowulf" does not in fact have a title to see how different matters are in these two cases.

If the New Testament is actually a tract put about by mushroom-eaters, we cannot leave the matter there. Other literature must be examined to see whether it may have been intended to convey a cryptic, esoteric message. Take Shakespeare's *Henry the Fifth.* On the face of it, here is a straightforward play on a national theme, so clear-cut and unexceptionable in its point of view and in most of its substance that it is regularly prescribed by "O" level examination boards. Every schoolboy has struggled to learn "Once more unto the breach, dear friends". The happy few and their achievements are echoed in Churchill's words about a later few who defended not the aggressive reputation of the English on foreign soil but the very existence of England in the face of onslaught from the air. Yet the more one considers *Henry the Fifth* in the light of Mr Allegro's philological inquiries, the more one wonders whether generation after generation of Englishmen have not been gulled by an author who never intended them to take his words at their face-value.

One of the features of *Henry the Fifth* that strikes any person on a second reading is the profusion of vegetable imagery. This is usually given an honourable mention along with such other features as the function of the Chorus and the credibility of the wooing scenes; it is regarded as imagery that enhances and should be recognised as such. But suppose the vegetable imagery is not secondary but primary? Suppose Shakespeare deliberately wrapped around a basic agricultural message a play that he knew would prove to be acceptably popular? A few minutes' attention to the play will convince an observant reader that the play does indeed conceal such a message. The first line "O for a muse of fire . . ." introduces what is on the face of it a straightforward wish for inspiration from the gods. But "muse" conceals another meaning; the "musa" in Shakespeare's time was the common name of the plantain or banana tree, and the banana is a straightforward phallic symbol. "Fire" suggests energy and power, sexual energy and power as much as any other. In the second scene of the first act occurs the long and tedious discourse by the Archbishop of Canterbury on the Salic law. Why should a competent playwright have included this long and dull exposition of an abstruse legal point; he must surely have known that it would send the audience to sleep? The answer is that the audience knew perfectly well that Shakespeare was not talking about the laws of succession; he was discussing under the thinnest of camouflages the merits of salep, an extract of orchid tubers. The word "salep" derives from an Arabic word meaning literally "fox's testicles". Shakespeare was in fact discussing the merits of salep as an aid to sexual potency, but he disguised it as a legal wrangle over the claim to the French throne. So one could continue. The play abounds in allusions to the power

51

of various herbs and weeds to increase sexual potency. I shall not weary readers with further details. It is in fact the easiest thing in the world to find a cryptic sexual message in *Henry the Fifth*. Henry himself is plainly a phallic hero, a symbol of maleness; covert sexual allusions abound. The more one looks for clues, the more clues one discovers. The result is an entirely new interpretation of an apparently straightforward play. Of course, nobody has interpreted *Henry the Fifth* along these lines hitherto, and there is no contemporary evidence that the audience understood it in these terms, but this only serves to show how promptly the Elizabethan and Jacobean governments acted in stamping out what must have been an underground sexual cult. Only accept the idea of a hidden message and everything can be explained – somehow.

Of course, if one reads *Henry the Fifth* in this way, it does rather spoil one's enjoyment of a traditional rendering of the play. One finds oneself continually becoming aware of possible sexual allusions. It is scarcely possible to take the play seriously as a study in war and kingship. A doubt about the author's intentions has been introduced to the reader's mind and it can never be altogether dismissed. Can it be that *Henry the Fifth* is but one example of a stream of literature that represents the interests of an erotic cult? Must we investigate all our major authors with the object of discovering whether their ostensible subject does not conceal esoteric statements on sex? The possibility must be considered.

The attribution of allegorical meanings (partial or fully developed) to ancient or modern literature is an activity like marriage "not by any to be enterprized, nor taken in hand, unadvisedly, lightly, or wantonly . . .; but reverently, discreetly, advisedly, soberly . . ." Activity of this kind all too easily leads the imagination captive. Matthew Prior's gambit in the lines

The merchant, to secure his treasure,
Conveys it in a borrow'd name:
Euphelia serves to grace my measure;
But Chloe is my real flame.

may serve to sustain a pleasing lyric, but more serious things are afoot in a collection of documents which purports to enshrine God's final revelation to his creatures. Much more is at stake than whether Euphelia is really Chloe. We want to know whether in Jesus we are confronting God's last word to man.

Mr Allegro is not a man for half-measures. He claims to have discovered a hidden message in the New Testament. The New Testament is not what we gullible Christians have all along supposed, the account of God's rescue operation conducted in the person of Christ his Son. The New Testament is not about anything so abstract and fanciful. It is a brochure for drug-takers; the "Christian" element is merely a thin piece of camouflage more startlingly successful than its authors ever dreamed it would be.

Mr Allegro's theory of hidden meaning is one that discredits the whole basis of Christianity. It is not that he is setting a question mark against a particular view of the Church as a supernaturally ordered society or against the Bible as an inspired revelation from God. What Mr Allegro is doing is to question the right of Christianity as we know it to exist at all. It is not whether Roman Catholics, or Anglicans, or Methodists, or radicals, or traditionalists are correct that is at issue in the light of the mushroom theory; what is at stake is whether or not Roman Catholics, Anglicans, Baptists and the rest are grossly and utterly deceived in all that they affirm. What they have in common is said to be no more than a fiction. It may be therefore that one side-effect of Mr Allegro's book will be to close the Christian ranks, to unite the Christians in affirming the historicity and authority of Christ.

Mr Allegro does not confine himself to the New Testament. He says for example that the whole Eden story is mushroom-based mythology, that it corresponds to other ancient garden-concepts, that it represents the mushroom as a source of delight. And the snake? The snake, of course, was a phallic symbol, sharing with the mushroom the uncommon habit of appearing unexpectedly out of the ground and bearing in its head a powerful poison which it was able to transfer to the mushroom and vice versa. Other passages in the Old Testament are dealt with by Mr Allegro; he regards early devotees of the mushroom cult as spinning endless verbal allusions to their revered fungus. But the main target Mr Allegro has in mind is the New Testament, for the New Testament, he says, was deliberately designed as a misleading cover story, whereas the Old Testament is more of a random jumble, a theological Tom Tiddler's Ground in which all can gain prizes.

The New Testament is, then, like *The Faerie Queene,* an allegory, but it is a tentative, incomplete, partial allegory. We do wrong to look for a meaning as complete, rounded and satisfying as that found under the surface of *Animal Farm.* After abandoning the traditional understanding of the New Testament we can expect nothing better than a few conspicuous coded messages, standing out like outcrops of rock in a ploughed field. On Mr Allegro's view the outcrops are everything and the ploughed field is nothing. We must reserve our attention for the outcrops that he believes to signify the hidden meaning now revealed after two thousand years of being lost to human sight.

And the factors that lead Mr Allegro to these conclusions? They come under two heads — philology and botany. The philological argument amounts to an assertion that key-words in Hebrew, Aramaic and Greek are developed from Sumerian words denoting the *amanita muscaria.* The botanical argument amounts to the identification of the *amanita muscaria* under its numerous popular designations as a potent fungus which was widely recognised to have unusual effects on those who consumed it. If it can be shown that certain words in the Old and New Testaments have been included in the text with the deliberate intention of drawing a reader's intention to the *amanita muscaria*, and if it can be shown that ancient writers intended to refer to the *amanita muscaria* when they appear to be referring to quite different plants, then we must accept Mr Allegro's theory that the New Testament has a hidden meaning which has now come to light after nineteen hundred years. If we cannot be satisfied on these two points, then the theory, however specious, must be discarded and added to the heap of theories which have offered a novel interpretation of the Bible, and have now found their way either into the history books or into the hands of one of the innumerable variations on orthodox Christianity that have gained some measure of popular if half-witted support.

John the Redcap

The name and title of "John the Baptist" in the New Testament story then, means no more than the "red-topped mushroom" . . .

John M. Allegro, *The Sacred Mushroom and the Cross*

If the New Testament contains a hidden meaning, how have the mushroom cult authors concealed their message? What must we look for? Where should we start? What kind of clues should we expect? We have after all been reading the New Testament for a long time without suspecting any ulterior significance. Mr Allegro makes the answer plain. To discover the hidden message we must give close attention to names, not to any of the numerous place names and people's names in the New Testament but to a few in particular. We must for example think carefully about the name of John the Baptist.

It is in the names of such people as John the Baptist that we find the mushroom cult making their most imaginative sallies. The compilers of what we call the New Testament did not, remember, invent new names as a way of alluding to particular characters then living who might resent such references; the compilers of the New Testament were not satirists half-afraid of the powerful men they were mocking. The mushroom men had another task in hand. They were concealing clues to the fly agaric, and their concern was to compose a literary work in which the clues could be embedded without causing undue suspicion. Their activity resembled that of the authorities in this country who during the 1939–45 war transmitted radio messages to French resistance groups under cover of harmless personal greetings and news. This kind of activity puts a premium on pure inventiveness; it demands the same qualities as are required of the script-writers who invest the

Archers with such thoroughgoing verisimilitude that these imaginary radio characters have more life and authenticity for some people than any living people except their immediate neighbours. The mushroom cult authors were equally inventive. Not the Archers but the Bar-Josephs and the Zebedees; not Ambridge, but Capernaum; the families and localities are different but the inventiveness is the same. Every so often, however, tucked inconspicuously into the story are camouflaged allusions to the fly agaric and to the cult that was based upon it.

John the Baptist is, on Mr Allegro's understanding of him, not "The last and greatest Herald of Heaven's King" — as William Drummond described him in a notable sonnet. He is no more than a solitary mushroom addict invented by the mushroom eaters to convey the name of their favourite fungus in half a dozen ways. The traditional Christian view of him as a man of fearless integrity who, for the sake of his devotion to duty spent all his life either in the desert or in prison must yield to a fanciful story dictated by the demands of word-play as inferior verse is shaped by the demands of rhyme. John the Baptist's name is nothing more than a camouflaged reference to the *amanita muscaria*. We should do better to call him John the Redcap. The name "John" comes, says Mr Allegro, from a Sumerian word GAN-NU, meaning red dye. The description "Baptist" comes from the hypothetical Sumerian word TAB-BA-R/LI, meaning mushroom. His camel's hair clothing (the camel, remember, has two humps, as the mushroom volva has two halves) conceals a reference to the mushroom because the Hebrew word for "camel" can be interpreted as a pun on the Greek word for "mandrake" (which plant Mr Allegro holds to be the *amanita muscaria*). The pun is substantiated by the fact that, according to Mr Allegro, both the Hebrew *kirkarah* and the Greek *kirkaia* come from a Sumerian root KUR-KUR, a name, he says, of the Holy Plant. Not only the clothing but the diet of John the Baptist is an allusion to the sacred mushroom.

The Semitic words for "locust" and "mushroom" are close enough in form for word-play to be possible; the closeness is accounted for by the fact that they both come from a Sumerian root meaning "pod" — indicating the larva in the case of the insect and the volva in the case of the mushroom. The story of the beheading of John is no more than a similarly elaborate exercise in providing clues leading the diligent reader to the fly agaric. "Baptist" and "platter" are both puns on the Sumerian mushroom-word TAB-BA-LI; "banquet for the men of Galilee", "unto half my kingdom", "bound in prison", "daughter of Herodias" are all expressions introduced into the story for the sake of the opportunities for word-play that they provide. If people are silly enough to take the preacher in the wilderness at his face value, they are at liberty to do so, but on Mr Allegro's view John the Baptist is merely a colourful (literally colourful) product of the mushroom men's imagination; the underlying purpose of his creators is to weave together allusions to the sacred mushroom.

The "sons of thunder" passage (Mark 3.17) is of crucial importance; it may even have been intended as a way into the subterranean caves of mushroom terminology concealed beneath the surface of the New Testament. The writer has here, as Mr Allegro understands it, gone to the trouble of providing a false explanation to a nickname. By doing so he presumably hoped to make his readers stop and think — and then uncover the entrance giving access to the subterranean terminology which was the real justification of the composition. The false explanation, says Mr Allegro, is in fact a fairly clear reference to the *amanita muscaria*, for it was known by this name ("son of thunder") among both Semitic and Greek speaking peoples. (It appeared mysteriously, remember, after rain — divine seed — had fallen to the earth.) What we have here is not a nickname given to two mettlesome brothers who were more than ready to call down fire on a Samaritan village that would not welcome Jesus and his friends (Luke 9.54); we have in the jumbled expression "Boanerges" which is "explained" in the Gospels, a phrase leading back to a hypothetical Sumerian compound GEShPU-AN-UR meaning "mighty man (holding up) the arch of heaven", a cosmographical reference to the mushroom in fact. A subterfuge of this kind, says Mr Allegro, puts the historicity and validity of the New Testament in jeopardy. If there is indeed subterfuge, then the point of the New Testament is not its face value story but the subterranean warren of mushroom references.

Mr Allegro makes much of this passage. If subterfuge can be proved at this point, he says, "the historicity and validity of the New Testament story is in ruins." What can we say to this? Are we to deny the possibility of any mushroom reference here and so preserve the historicity and validity of the New Testament? Can we do this? The answer is that we cannot. We can only say that we do not know what the text means at this point. Mr Allegro and other Semitic experts must argue the point out. As far as the Cambridge Greek Testament Commentary on Mark goes, the word "Boanerges" is held to be a corrupt transliteration of an Aramaic or Hebrew phrase; C.E.B. Cranfield, the commentator, suggests three possible Hebrew or Aramaic words that might lie behind the phrase – the first meaning agitation, the second anger, the third commotion. Plainly this is a field for scholarly speculation rather than straightforward information of the kind needed by people with trains to catch and unfamiliar equipment to handle. Equally plainly it is hazardous to base a novel theory on one possible understanding of the text at this point. More evidence than this is needed before caution gives way to enthusiastic demolition and reconstruction work.

The apostle Peter is another character brought into being by the mushroom cult author. He has been given a name which is an obvious play, says Mr Allegro, on the Semitic word *pitra*, meaning mushroom. His patronymic, Bar-jona, is cognate with the Greek word *paionia*, meaning paeony. Both, says Mr Allegro, may be traced to a hypothetical Sumerian word BAR-IA-U-NA. On the occasion of the Great Confession Peter is called a stumbling-block, but this of course is yet another allusion to the mushroom for *tiqla* is the bolt-mushroom name meaning bolt-plant to which we shall refer later. On the same occasion Peter is called "Satan" and both this and the name "Cephas" are allusions to the mushroom. (In Greek and Latin the onion is called *setanion* or *setania*, as is also the medlar, and there is also a Latin word *caepa* from which is derived the French word *cepe* or *ceps*, meaning mushroom.) Here then is another character introduced into the Gospel story for the sake of acting as a vehicle for mushroom information. And the information? Well, says Mr Allegro, none other than the keys that were given to him, for the keys represent the fly agaric opening the door to exciting new mystical experiences. Even this is not the end of the word-play for the passage about the keys has a Sumerian basis, the hypothetical compound MASh-BA(LA)G-ANTA-TAB-BA-RI.

It scarcely needs saying that if Mr Allegro is right about Peter's name, then all the arguing over whether Peter was the first Pope and whether he and his successors in that office have the power to open and shut the gates of heaven when men and women apply for admission is so much hot air. It is all a misunderstanding. Men died at the stake, bigots ranted and roared, moderate men bowed their heads in shame, and all the time they would have been better occupied playing bowls or dancing round the maypole. They were disputing, straining their mental powers and dying over things that had never existed. Whether their allegiance was to the Pope, to Martin Luther or to the Queen of England their excitement was groundless. They would have done better to dismiss from their minds all thoughts of divine revelation and to agree that there was nothing in

Christianity to detain any man longer than it would take him to say "fly agaric". They were no different from "the heathen in his blindness" who "bows down to wood and stone". Heathen and Christian alike were mistaken about the nature of God. Whether a man was a Protestant or Papist mattered little, for both were deceived, grossly, irremediably deceived. Peter and the keys never existed; the massive turn of events that we call the Protestant Reformation was an argument over nothing more substantial than a mushroom. Everybody concerned might have spared himself the trouble.

Barnabas loses his position as an admirable purveyor of encouragement and is seen to be yet another example of the punner's inventiveness. The name "Barnabas" is not Aramaic at all; it is a development of a Sumerian compound meaning giraffe-skin — i.e. skin with red and white spots — and indicates the *amanita muscaria*. As for the apostle's first name, Joseph, that comes from a hypothetical Sumerian compound meaning "Yahweh (semen)-penis". The "explanation" provided in the text, "Son of Encouragement" also points to the *amanita muscaria*, if in a rather more roundabout fashion. Barnabas was a native of Cyprus. The Aramaic word *kuphra* is near enough to the Greek word for Cyprus to make a pun feasible. *Kuphra* signifies the red dye henna. Red is the colour of the glans penis. Cyprus was seen by the ancients as a penis about to penetrate the eastern end of the Mediterranean. What more could a literary agent of the mushroom sect want?

By comparison the orthodox view of Barnabas is rich, robust and engaging. When we pick out his story from the texture of the New Testament story, we find a man of independent mind who was not in the least deterred at the thought of vouching for the newly converted Paul amongst suspicious Christians in Jerusalem. When others hung back shamefaced at the thought of accepting this fair-seeming Pharisee, Barnabas put his reputation at risk and introduced him to the other leaders of the Church as an honest believer in Christ. Later, Barnabas showed just as much loyalty to young John Mark in the face of Paul's opposition. When Paul declined to take the risk of campaigning with a doubtful colleague (as John Mark had once shown himself to be), Barnabas would not budge. If John Mark could not go, he was not going either. Neither Paul nor Barnabas would yield, so Paul went one way with a new colleague, Silas, and Barnabas went another way with John Mark. It is this steadfastness, this readiness to stand by another person when the opposition is strong that makes Barnabas so winning a member of the Christian team in Acts. If Barnabas was a mere invention, if he is nothing more than a peg on which to hang a giraffe-skin, then he was an inspired invention that has nerved many in subsequent generations to stick to their guns.

But if John the Baptist, Peter, James and John and Barnabas were key figures in the coded writings, they were all eclipsed by the prime mushroom symbol, Jesus himself. Jesus, born of a virgin, was the mushroom-worshippers' way of describing the uniquely begotten mushroom, mysteriously and unpredictably showing itself after the god had poured semen into the earth during a thunderstorm. More than any other form of plant life, the tiny mushroom was the god manifest, a miniature of the mighty originating penis which (who?) had brought the world into being. What better could represent this miniature in an allegory than a living person who likewise had had an unaccountable birth? The name Jesus, ultimately cognate with the name Dionysus (Bacchus), comes from a hypothetical Sumerian word meaning "semen which saves"; it is a camouflaged term for the sacred mushroom. The name Christ (or Messiah), meaning "anointed", is a reference to the divine semen or mushroom juice with which the cult leaders were anointed.

The allegory asserts itself in other matters than the name of

65

Jesus. A cross, says Mr Allegro, particularly a cross with a peg to support the victim at the crotch, is a euphemistic reference to sexual copulation. The expression "Christ crucified", which to the Christian stands for all that is most sacred to him, represents on Mr Allegro's view the semen-anointed, erect mushroom. The occurrence of this phrase in I Corinthians 1.22 is merely a piece of trans-lingual word-play involving both Aramaic and Greek expressions for the fungus. The Jews call it a bolt-plant; the Greeks call it a mushroom (similar to the Greek word for "folly"). As before, those who wish to do so can take this verse at its face value and say that it represents different attitudes in the ancient world to the death of Christ on the cross for man's sins. The enlightened people who know that it is the subterranean meaning that is important will see here the much more significant reference to the mushroom. The crucifixion of Jesus is, after all, no more than a story conceived and written to provide opportunities for word-play like this.

But the crucifixion of Christ has meant more than this to countless people. It meant more than this to the drug-addict's mother mentioned in Bruce Kenrick's *Come out the Wilderness* (Fontana). "Think of Jesus hanging on the Cross," she said to a congregation. "Remember how he shouted out, 'My God, why have you forsaken me?' Well, that's understood by the addict . . ." Kenrick goes on: "This mother understood the cry as well, for she had suffered with her son. Ray's pastor and his lay church friends also understood the cry, for they were suffering with him." It is impossible to deny to those who have suffered deeply the right to speak of the authenticity of what they know of the sufferings of Christ on the cross. If life means anything at all, an understanding of suffering is an important part of the meaning, and often an awareness of the importance of Christ's death on the cross is an important part of human understanding of the matter. Of course, a Christian believer

66

will wish to say more about the cross than this. He will wish to say with Paul that Christ Jesus came into the world to save sinners. He will say that he is dead and his life is hid with Christ in God. He will say that in Christ he is living a new life. There are countless people in the world today who would say that any goodness there is in their lives comes from an encounter with Christ crucified, ascended and risen. When so many lives have been made fragrant and meaningful and the people concerned name Christ as the author of all that is most meaningful in life, one has to balance such testimony against puns and fungus.

Once the entrance to the subterranean warren of meaning has been found, the perceptive reader with the necessary philological equipment and a keen scent finds mushroom imagery everywhere. What we know as the Lord's prayer is a ritual performance associated with this dangerous plant. The petitions are riddled with puns on the name of the fungus. Jesus' cry of desertion on the cross is no more than the incantation used by mushroom worshippers to ease the plant's removal from the ground (or to encourage it to show itself). Jesus' comment on the Ten Commandments? Merely an occasion to slip in a few more cryptic references to mushrooms. And the Ten Commandments themselves? A mushroom myth with the two tablets representing the two halves of the mushroom volva. The Old Testament, however, is not the neat and orderly composition that the New Testament is; in the Old Testament mushroom worshippers and their enemies jostle for column inches: it is not so easy to disentangle one from the other.

Among those whose reputations are now in ruins as a result of Mr Allegro's philological burrowings is Bacchus. He whom we had taken to be the god of wine and merriment is no more than the centre of a mushroom cult. His followers were not inflamed to revelry by alcohol but by *amanita muscaria*. The vine cluster that bears the same relation to the Bacchic cult as the cross bears to Christianity is now exposed as a representation of the tip of the penis. The beverage used at their orgies was no ordinary wine but wine sprinkled with powdered mushroom-tops. The vine imagery of which the Bacchic enthusiasts were fond is paralleled by the vine imagery applied to Christ in the fourth Gospel. What we did not know about the incantations used by the worshippers of Bacchus can now be supplied from such expressions in the New Testament as: "Awake, sleeper! Arise from the dead, and the Christ will give you light!" The cries uttered by the awed Bacchus mushroom worshippers are concealed by the New Testament writers under the form: "Eloi, Eloi, lama sabachthani!"

The strange thing about the New Testament as interpreted by Mr Allegro is that the numerous characters and incidents he processes prove to have a weary sameness about them. Whereas John Bunyan's story is full of characters who are different from one another and who represent different virtues and vices, Mr Allegro's interpretation is stale, flat and monotonous. Once we have discovered what John the Baptist is said to represent we need trouble ourselves no further. The next character to be dealt with will represent exactly the same thing. The answer in each case is a mushroom. Instead of diversity and humanity there is uniformity and predictability. John the Baptist is a mushroom. James and John are mushrooms. Peter is a mushroom. Barnabas is a mushroom. Jesus is a mushroom. In Mr Allegro's hands the essence of the New Testament becomes something we can see, touch and smell. It is all nothing more or less than a warty-topped red and white mushroom. When we hold this in our hands we are master of more wisdom than that attained by other men who lack the secret. We are grasping a truth that has consistently eluded generations of patient scholars and students of the Bible. Under the brightly coloured rind is the secret of religious perception. John the Baptist and his fellows are mere camouflage. This is the view Mr Allegro invites us adopt..

The best-kept secret

I have done one braver thing
Than all the Worthies did,
And yet a braver thence doth spring,
Which is, to keep that hid.

John Donne, *The Undertaking*

If we are to accept the sacred mushroom as the key to a right understanding of the Jewish and Christian Scriptures, we must accept the view that the correct interpretation of the Scriptures has been hidden for nineteen hundred years and has only come to light in 1970. If in fact Mr Allegro is correct, then the sacred mushroom is the best kept secret in the history of the human race. The man who is going to take this view must be prepared to accept a conspiracy so cunning, so convincing, so completely ordered in all its details that no whisper of it leaked out to make the leadership of the Jews and of the new-born Christian movement suspect that they were setting off on a wild goose chase by talking of a Messiah who would deliver his people from their sins. The apostle Paul, the New Testament writers, those who preserved the tales of Jesus and passed them on by word of mouth, all were entirely deceived about the nature of the religion they were promulgating (though some of them may have been party to the conspiracy). What they thought was an appearing of the Son of God with authority and power was merely a fiction to conceal an aphrodisiac recipe. What they took to be an actual historical event outside Jerusalem when God's Son took human sin and suffering upon himself was no more than a trimming added to the essential coded message. Those men who were not conspirators and forgers were entirely misled. Consummate deception was followed by crass gullibility. The deception died away and was forgotten; the gullibility was perpetuated through generation

71

after generation until Mr Allegro demonstrated how thoroughly the whole of Europe had been deceived for nineteen hundred years. The man who is going to accept Mr Allegro's theory must accept this.

When the Duke of Wellington was accosted by a man in the street with the words "Mr Jones, I believe" the Duke is supposed to have replied: "If you believe that you will believe anything." The act of faith required to accept that a secret so profound, so enormous in its consequences if disclosed, so powerful as a means of self-advancement, so formidable a weapon against one's enemies should have been kept with such success for so long is an act of faith so great that compared with the act of faith necessary to accept the truth of the Christian Gospel it is like Mount Everest compared with Ludgate Hill. However tempted one might be on purely philological grounds to accept the truth of Mr Allegro's hypothesis, one would have to swallow not a gnat but a camel as one went on to agree that all the Christians who have ever lived have been grossly, palpably, laughably deceived by the instigators of the great mushroom hoax. There is a time to acknowledge one's mistakes, innumerable as they often are, and there is a time to concede one's point when formidable arguments are marshalled against one, but there is also time to smile when a specious theory is so bold and so extravagant as to defy rational argument. Such a theory is the one Mr Allegro puts before us. It is as though a man were to argue that the invention of the wheel was the result of a plot laid by wicked men to keep the human race occupied while they performed their nefarious business; the wheel proved so absorbing and determinative in human history that man has neglected to inquire whether it did not in fact divert his attention from more important things. Or it is as though a man were to argue that the invention of writing was put about by a power-hungry tribal leader who then went on to perform his *coup d'état* to his own satisfaction

72

while his less intelligent contemporaries were arguing the merits of lower case against capitals; the matter of writing proved so absorbingly interesting that the poor new literates did not realise that they had been deprived of their rights by a more astute chieftain than themselves. Both these things may be true, and indeed, there may be societies dedicated to propounding these theories and gaining supporters for them, just as there are Flat-earthers at work today, but as far as most of us are concerned, there are more important things to argue about. Whatever the putative plotters may have got up to, the wheel and the practice of writing have proved of such inestimable benefit to the course of civilised life on this planet that any fracas surrounding their origin has been completely eclipsed by their undoubted utility.

Of course the suspicious man finds conspiracies everywhere. He suspects local authorities of being in league with motor car manufacturers because the yellow lorries with the flashing lights cover the winter roads with so much corrosive salt that cars quickly have to be replaced. The editorial columns of newspapers are suspect because no newspaper can afford to upset a big advertiser whose product the newspaper is commenting upon. The parent who is unable to gain a place for his child at the school of his choice is convinced that the headmasters concerned and the divisional education officer are working hand in glove. Nobody could deny that there is occasionally a grain of truth in one or more of these examples, but it is all too easy to find secrets, plots and cabals once a search for them is begun. It is also one of the hardest things in the world to keep a genuine secret, and when Mr Allegro asks us to believe that the secret message of the New Testament has remained undiscovered for nearly two thousand years he is asking us to fly in the face of probability and to believe that an altogether desirable product should have been kept from common use and only now been discovered.

We have only to compare the fly agaric with the vine to see how great are the odds against secrecy being preserved in the case of the former. It was early discovered that the fermented juice of the grape cheered the heart of man and made him more convivial. The discovery of alcohol and its properties must have been one of the great milestones in human history. A monopoly of wine production could have assured for the successful viniculturist a life of security and prosperity. Yet the juice of the grape became an open secret, and the cultivation of the vine became one of the most widespread occupations of agricultural man. The grape is not as potent as the fly agaric, but both the fly agaric and the grape yield poisonous products, both affect the nervous systems, both affect the taker's powers of perception, both subdue his fears. If one should have been favoured with secrecy, why not the other? If men today are only too eager to ferret out what others are trying to keep to themselves, why were men yesterday so different? If men today are foolish enough to experiment with dangerous drugs in order to enjoy their benefits, why were men not equally foolish two thousand and more years ago?

Or again, why should knowledge of the fly agaric have been suppressed whilst knowledge of the tobacco plant became available on a world-wide scale? It was doubtless alarming for the first Europeans to see the indigenous inhabitants of the Americas stuffing a roll of leaf up their nostrils, lighting the other end and happily drawing the smoke down into their lungs. Yet some brave European souls ventured to do the same and found the result gratifying. It was not long before a cigar in the mouth or a pipe was found to be more convenient than a leaf in the nose, but the courage (even if we think it was misguided) of those pioneers must be recognised. It is only today that we are beginning to discover the dangerous properties of the tobacco plant, yet it is impossible to imagine the secret of it being preserved once the first European had caught sight of this curious plant being enjoyed.

However great the sanctions, religious or civil, designed to warn men off secrets which the few wish to keep to themselves, the task of preserving the secrecy of a particularly potent discovery is peculiarly difficult. Printing, steam-power, jet propulsion, nuclear energy have all been discovered by the few and developed by the many. The secret weapon remains secret only until the enemy are found to have the same secret or a better one themselves.

From the Molly Maguires of Ireland and Pennsylvania to the Foresters and Odd Fellows of England history is full of well documented societies with secrets. Few have managed to preserve their secrets against the unceasing inquisitiveness of their fellow-men. Those that have must as often as not give the credit to their neighbours' lack of curiosity about secrets that are reckoned to be vain rather than to any successful measures to ensure continued secrecy. The newspaper reporter in his dirty raincoat is symbolic of man's unfading lust for news and information about the world around him, for a way into other people's secrets — provided those secrets are worth knowing.

In 1896 rich gold-bearing gravels were discovered along Bonanza Creek in the Klondike. Within the next three or four years thirty thousand people had poured into this inhospitable —and almost inaccessible — area. By 1900 the output of gold had reached an annual level of twenty-two million dollars. The gold rush added a new word to our vocabulary and led amongst other things to a classic Charlie Chaplin comedy and to the near-documentary material of Jack London and Robert Service. Perhaps the first man to strike it rich had dreams of keeping it all to himself; it never worked out that way. Men fell over one another to be first to the gold-field. Harsh though the region might be, it failed to intimidate those who had heard about the strike from afar; they did not want to be left out if gold was to be found.

In 1869 the "Star of South Africa", an 83½ carat diamond, was purchased by the Earl of Dudley for twenty-five thousand pounds. The stone had been found near the Orange river. By 1870 a mining camp with a population of ten thousand people was established in the vicinity. In that year and the following year diamonds were discovered in the neighbourhood of Kimberley. In no time at all fifty thousand people had been drawn to the township, which rapidly developed from a tented camp to a permanent town named after the then Secretary of State for the Colonies.

In 1517 a Spaniard, Francisco de Cordoba, with twenty-five of his men, landed on the coast of what we now call Mexico and discovered the first masonry buildings to be seen by white men in the New World. The gold ornaments that they discovered in these houses from which the occupants had fled were evidence of the achievements of the Maya civilisation, a civilisation notable for its skill in mathematics, astronomy, architecture and engineering. The lure of gold drew more and more Spaniards to Mexico — among them Hernando Cortes. The Aztec empire was destroyed in the course of his determined invasion, but at the end of the day there was little gold to reward his followers. The great promise which had lured men across the Atlantic finally proved to be hollow, but it was a powerful magnet attracting those Europeans who were looking to the New World for riches beyond their dreams.

Can we possibly believe that once it was known that there was gold in the Klondike, or diamonds in South Africa, or treasures in Mexico the news could be suppressed and secrecy preserved? In all these places and in the royal tombs of Egypt the possibility of discovering treasure has been sufficient incentive to persuade men to risk their lives in discovering or recovering hidden wealth. Hidden treasure there must be in various parts of the world, buried under the ground, concealed in wrecked galleons, but it only remains untouched when it is not feasible to locate and extract it.

There have of course been pieces of information which have slipped out of sight in the course of history. The Romans' method of making concrete was lost to Europeans for centuries and the Chinese way with porcelain was lost to view and never recovered. There were discoveries which were never properly exploited – the Greek invention of the steam engine which never became more than a toy, the Chinese fire-crackers which were never developed for industrial purposes, the many ideas of Leonardo da Vinci's which remained on the drawing-board. Rarely, however, has a significant breakthrough been lost to sight altogether; man's curiosity is too great to allow that to happen. The more closely men's interests are bound up with a particular piece of knowledge, the less likely they are to allow it to disappear. When the matter is one that concerns their sexual activity, the likelihood of one man or a group of men keeping a secret to themselves is remote indeed.

So fearful and formidable were the powers of the hallucinatory poisons concealed beneath the skin of the magic mushroom, writes Mr Allegro, that no man who had been initiated into the secret dared to write it down. Instead he passed it on surreptitiously and fearfully, with many a wary glance over his shoulder, to another man thought worthy of sharing the secret. So scrupulous were the first century possessors of this secret about not committing the secret to writing that knowledge of the secret died out; men forgot the secret of the mushroom. Now what we are being invited to consider in this connexion is the possibility that this secret would never find its way on to paper – or papyrus or clay. We can best weigh up this possibility by recalling how officers and other ranks during the first world war successfully kept diaries while they were in the front line despite all the prohibitions and penalties announced by the generals to deter the diarists. The incentive for keeping a war diary was as nothing compared with the incentive to make sure of preserving the mushroom secret. A drug that would guide its devotee through simulated sexual ecstasy into a taste of eternal bliss is a drug that a man would break any regulation for. As well might we entertain the possibility that man would allow the knowledge of alcohol to perish from the face of the earth, that man would allow himself to overlook the grape or the barleycorn. That man should be able to keep the sacred mushroom secret strains credibility far enough; that he should allow himself to forget about it is to impose so great a burden on credibility that few men of common sense will be able to treat the suggestion seriously.

When in 1856 William Henry Smith put in a claim on behalf of Francis Bacon to authorship of the plays generally credited to Shakespeare he was not the first to make that claim. The Rev James Wilmot, of Warwickshire, is said to have suggested the possibility of Bacon's authorship of the plays in 1785. Smith argued the case; Delia Bacon popularised it in a book published the following year, 1857. Soon the Bacon Society was founded to further this view of the matter and the Baconian authorship of Shakespeare's plays has been given a frequent airing ever since.

The Baconian theory has plausible points. We know next to nothing of Shakespeare's life, whereas we know that Francis Bacon was a man of great intelligence and capability. But the case lacks positive evidence — just as the view that the Earl of Oxford or the Earl of Rutland wrote the works of Shakespeare lacks positive evidence. What some supporters of the Baconian case have strongly supported is the presence of a cipher message hidden in Shakespeare's works giving evidence of Bacon's authorship.

It may be thought that to replace Shakespeare by Bacon is a big enough step to cause a stir. But after the initial excitement had died down interest waned; everybody came to accept the fact that there was a group of Bacon supporters; they collected footnotes in the standard works on Shakespeare; but Shakespeare studies carried on as though nothing had happened. After all, what is important is the text, and the merits of the text are so commanding that discussion of cryptic messages and the like is a matter of walking and peeping about around the legs of a Colossus. The same consequence is likely to follow Mr Allegro's announcement. Some who read his book will become enthusiastic advocates of his point of view; an enclave of mushroom theorists will have been inaugurated; but the majority of those who take their Bibles seriously will continue to take the plain merits and general coherence of the text as more convincing than a novel interpretation based on a few selected passages.

Some secrets have indeed been well kept in the course of man's history. Of particular interest are the secrets of the mystery religions. We have little information about the rituals and procedures of these groups and what we do know about them has been deduced from architectural remains as much as from surviving documents. We know that various rites were followed, and that the mysteries that took place under the auspices of Demeter were different from the mysteries presided over by Mithras or one of the Egyptian deities. The blood of bulls or pigs and the display of phallic emblems had a more or less prominent part in the proceedings. To a greater or lesser extent there was a similarity to the doctrines of Christianity, with a place for death and resurrection, atonement etc. Drama or pageant may have been at the heart of the matter. Holy objects were perhaps displayed before initiates, and it may be that they took the form of a fertility symbol. Sharing in a sacred cup was another likely part of the proceedings. Some mysteries were marked by orgiastic abandon.

Here then is a type of secret, and a particularly relevant secret, which has successfully been preserved. If this type of mystery could preserve its secret, why could not the mushroom sect preserve the secret of the fly agaric? Indeed, is it not possible that the real secret of the mystery religions was nothing but the fly agaric? Is it not possible that Apuleius, whose hero coyly declines to be specific about the initiation which he underwent at the end of *The Golden Ass*, was introduced to the fly agaric? Are there not grounds for thinking that all the fertility cults — including the "Christian" one — were assiduously preserving the same secret, the potent, fearsome, sacred mushroom?

In connection with the mystery religions we must consider at least two possibilities. In the first place it is possible that the mystery religions as a whole, like the sect responsible for the New Testament, made the fly agaric the centre of their activities. In that case credibility is strained even further. Not one mystery religion, but a multitude of mystery religions were guardians of the great and awful secret. It was not merely one Judaean sect that managed to preserve the secret; the same feat was achieved by numerous other bodies. To accept that secrecy was successfully preserved when groups all over the Empire were addicted to the fly agaric is to sin against probability without restraint. Here were men enjoying a drug that brought bliss and fulfilment; it was readily available under the pine trees; yet the knowledge of it faded from men's minds or was lost through failure to ensure that the secret was passed on.

The other possibility is that the adherents of the mystery religions managed to preserve their secrets because the secrets were of no great interest to anybody else. It is not unknown for men to make much of spurious formulae and rituals, or to inflate minor matters beyond their proper importance. In this case what was lost to subsequent generations was equivalent to the knowledge of the correct method of forming fours or piling arms, or to the slogans chanted by football supporters at White Hart Lane. We do not know which of these possibilities corresponds to the truth. We are not likely to know. We must be guided by our common sense.

What happened in the mushroom cult? We are to imagine newcomers being introduced under the vow of secrecy and with all the trappings to suggest supernatural powers close at hand to an experience of tasting the drug that leads straight to God. After a nervous nibble or gulp the novice would break into a sweat, be aware of flashing lights and see everything as though from a distance. Further visits to the shrine would lead to an increased dosage and to more intense hallucinatory experiences. All the time the novice would approach the experience with trepidation. He was after all tampering with the life-principle behind the universe. A false or temerarious step might stretch him dead before his fellow-worshippers. But as the novice turned into the practised drug-taker and as the regular worshipper moved up in the hierarchy, familiarity would begin to breed contempt. Desire for the drug would outweigh caution. Instead of obtaining his supplies from the regular religious source the worshipper would be tempted to collect his own mushrooms. What tends to happen in all activities would happen in this one. The mushroom worshipper would not be mysteriously exempt from the waning of enthusiasm that afflicts followers of all religions. Every mushroom picker who took his drug privately as well as in the course of religious service would represent a possible leak of secret information.

If other mystery religions made use of fly agaric, why did not those Roman officials who happened to be worshippers of Bacchus suspect that the dreaded phallic mushroom might be at the heart of the Christian movement too? Why were informers not infiltrated into the movement? How could the authorities be so dull and supine as to fail to penetrate the secrets of this dangerous sect? It would be widely known to men of affairs that devotees of the sacred mushroom characteristically presented a security risk. Instead of quietly enjoying flashing

81

lights and telescopic vision, they might turn to frenzied violence. A drug capable of turning men into what a later generation would call berserkers was a drug that state security systems could not afford to ignore.

The use of fly agaric is scarcely consistent with regular religious rituals. If fly agaric can turn a man into an assassin or berserker, any kind of communal drug-taking is likely to have disastrous consequences. A mystery religion that proved as noisy as the Hell-fire Club is unlikely to continue proof against neighbours' curiosity.

This all-purpose drug served to kill flies, to send men into combat regardless of consequences, to provide pleasurable experiences surpassing those of physical orgasm, to give them an illusion of spiritual resurrection. What sanction would be powerful enough to contain this secret once its initial discovery had been made? What power could prevent men accidentally discovering its properties if it was successfully cornered for religious purposes? Man has always been ready to experiment with traditional drugs such as narcotics and with new drugs such as LSD. The queue of people eager to become addicts is a guarantee that the secret of any potent drug will be very hard to keep. Is it possible to imagine the knowledge of LSD being stamped out by authorities aware of its dangers?

From the child daring to taste the berries in the hedgerow to the teenager taking LSD, from the days of the Queen of Sheba to the days of Mata Hari, from the days of Greek fire to the days of guided missiles, men have shown themselves chronically unable to keep a secret. Given sufficient gold, a sufficiently attractive Delilah, or a present or past favourable to blackmail, a man will divulge any secret. Rarely do men keep secrets deliberately. When secrets are preserved it is more often through chance or accident. The secret is buried beneath the ash of Pompeii or lost for ever among the forests of Brazil or simply not exploited by a race that is more interested in sculpture than in steam-power. To suppose that a drug of proven worth, as powerful as opium, as pleasurable as tobacco, as easily come by as alcohol should simply fade from sight or be utilised only by rare characters like berserkers and assassins is to suppose a change in human nature that passes credibility. Yet this is a supposition Mr Allegro invites us to make and if this supposition is not granted, his fly agaric theory is in ruins.

Jubilant code-cracker

It is now possible to propose combinations of known root elements with a fair degree of assurance; nevertheless the asterisk will appear frequently in the following pages and serve to remind us that such reconstructions, however probable, must find adequate cross-checking through the cognate languages if they are to be anything but speculative.

John M. Allegro, *The Sacred Mushroom and the Cross*

The number of men and women who will be able to make an authoritative assessment of Mr Allegro's philological findings is very small. It will therefore in all probability be some time before any worthwhile detailed comment on Mr Allegro's assertions about the Sumerian language is forthcoming. But even the layman can see that on Mr Allegro's own admission the number of Sumerian texts available is small and the proportion of speculative word-forms proposed by him in the course of his book is high. The proper course for a person innocent of Sumerian is to reserve judgment and take note of the fact that there is no evidence yet of an expert in Sumerian taking Mr Allegro's work seriously.

It may, however, be worthwhile pointing out that there are exceptional hazards confronting the man who makes a study of etymology. Things are not always what they seem. Who, for instance, with a name like Gibb or Gibbs would think that it was a diminutive form of Gilbert, meaning a tom-cat; Who would imagine that Ramsey meant "wild-garlic island", from the Old English "hramsa" (now ramson) meaning wild garlic, and "eye" meaning island?

"Paraffin" must surely, we think, have an honourable ancestry — Greek, perhaps? But no. The word "paraffin" was invented by a German scientist, Karl von Reichenbach in 1830. Having invented the stuff, he thought himself entitled to give it a name, so he did. He put together two Latin words "parum" and "affinis" because the new mixture of hydrocarbons had little affinity with other bodies.

The most learned people thought until comparatively recently that the word "abominable" came from the two Latin words *ab* and *homine*; the plausible explanation was offered that the word meant "away from man, inhuman". An intrusive "h" therefore maintained its place in the spelling of the word with no justification whatever. When we read *Paradise Lost*, we are surprised to find the word "sovereign" spelled "sovran", but this is a much more sensible spelling for a word derived from the Latin *superanus* than the form which has now established itself. Frequently it happens that things are not what they seem and of no field of human inquiry is this more true than of etymology. The first thing one learns about the development of place-names, for example, is the wisdom of making no kind of assertion about a place-name unless one has consulted a reference book and is reasonably sure of one's ground. The question of place-names abounds in pitfalls to trap the unwary speculator.

The slightest experience also teaches one to be extremely wary about concluding that an etymological meaning was present to the user of the particular word under consideration at any point in its history. We speak of the crocodile, for instance, without pausing for a moment to reflect that its name means "worm of the stones"; when we put on wellington boots or eat a sandwich we do not pause to pay tribute to the peers whose ideas we are utilising; we refer to a rocket and it does not cross our minds that the word "rocket" comes from a diminutive of the word "rock" (of unknown origin) meaning a distaff; we have our car-tank filled with petrol without thinking of the two Greek words for rock oil which have been abbreviated in common parlance. Words become rubbed smooth in use just as coins do; and just as one sometimes finds a coin rubbed so smooth that nothing of its original inscription remains, so one can find words of which the original meaning has been lost altogether. We speak of a throttle in a car, without recalling the act of strangling; we speak of nostrils and we do not call to mind nose-holes; we speak of admirals without thinking of emirs. Yet if we were required to stand to the etymology of what we were saying in everyday expressions we should find ourselves altogether flummoxed. When a driving instructor tells his pupil to press gently on the throttle to increase the flow of petrol through the carburettor, he is really telling his pupil to press gently on the stranglehold so as to increase the flow of rock-oil through the device for forming a compound with carbon. When we put a film into a camera we put a membrane or pellicle into a darkened chamber or box.

We do not of course use language in this etymological fashion. It is an interesting study to discover the remote origins of common words and one could spend an hour at less worthwhile pursuits than tracing the extraordinary history of such English words as harlot, galoshes, maudlin, lynch and ha-ha. However, we do not in fact stop to think of the sex change that has overtaken the word "harlot" any more than we think of Captain William Lynch of Pittsylvania, Virginia, when we refer to punishment imposed by a self-constituted court. We use the words in their current meaning and we are not bothered about their history. If a philologist interpreted our spoken and written words etymologically we should tell him that the ideas he was attributing to us had not entered our minds. He, if he was candid, would confess that he had not for one moment imagined that they had; he was just playing a little game with us.

To discover etymological meanings in words can be an engrossing pursuit, but what is important if one is studying the significance of the words at any particular time is to know how far the prior history of a word was consciously present to any person using it. If the person speaking or writing the word was

89

entirely oblivious of its history — as frequently happens with us today — then the etymology is no more than an academic trophy, interesting, decorative, but of no utility for present purposes. Puns that are dependent upon this kind of etymological inquiry are of little significance. One could find etymological puns everywhere. And as far as pun-makers are concerned, the greatest of these is Shakespeare.

"The Age in which the Punn chiefly flourished," writes Joseph Addison in *The Spectator*, No. 61, "was the Reign of King James the First ... The greatest Authors, in their most serious works, made frequent use of Punns. The Sermons of Bishop Andrews, and the Tragedies of Shakespear are full of them. The Sinner was punned into Repentance by the former, as in the latter nothing is more usual than to see a Hero weeping and quibbling for a dozen Lines together." The preacher or dramatist who has a punning turn of mind will scarcely be able to avoid word-play in the course of his sermons, just as John Donne could not avoid word-play on his own name in his most serious poetry. It is equally true that the reader or listener who has been fed a diet of puns will be on the watch for them at all times and will sometimes find them where they were never intended. In the matter of puns as in other things, "the appetite grows by eating." The man who has tuned his ear to perceive the faintest of puns is certain to find them; he may at the same time miss more important things.

There is a difference, however, between puns introduced as Shakespeare introduced them, to add an extra level of delight to plays which were already pleasurable as they stood, and puns which are fundamental to the understanding of a literary work the worth of which may be of relatively little consequence compared with the puns themselves. In the case of Shakespeare the puns are casually built into the play; in the case of the New Testament (as Mr Allegro understands it) the

Gospels, Epistles, etc. exist entirely for the sake of the puns. It is the puns which are the justification of the work.

Mr Allegro finds, as we have said, that the passage in I Corinthians chapter one about "Christ crucified, a stumbling-block to Jews and folly to Gentiles" is a piece of word-play alluding to the Aramaic and Greek terms for the sacred mushroom. The Greek word *skandalon*, like its Aramaic equivalent *tiqla*, originally meant "bolt", and "bolt" signifies the mushroom because of the phallic shape of both a bolt (or stick) and a mushroom. When the writer says that Christ crucified is a stumbling-block to the Jews, Mr Allegro would have us believe that he means to indicate the name by which the Jews know the sacred mushroom. The Greeks, on the other hand, know the mushroom as the *morios*, so the writer does the best he can by way of indicating the Greek term for the sacred mushroom and says the Greeks see Christ crucified to be "folly" (Greek *moria*). If one is determined to find puns in the New Testament because one has a theory which depends upon them, then puns such as these will probably serve the purpose, but suppose the writers of the New Testament meant what they said. Suppose they were not interested in puns or remote resemblances demanding an alert etymological sense. Suppose they meant that the Jews were always expecting miracles whilst the Greeks were always looking for intellectual brilliance, but the Gospel was the good news of a crucified Messiah. The etymologist can discover puns in the writings of any man who writes under the impetus of conviction, but this does not mean that the puns were intended by the writer in the first place.

Of course Mr Allegro is going back to the original formation of words in picture form. One cannot go further back than that. We must take his word as an expert on the question of interpreting the pictures, but we are not obliged to take his word about the question of those who used the picture-words assenting to their original implication. One has to take a language as one finds it when one wants to say something. A man who wants to get his message across is wise if he invents as few new words as possible to do so. That a word from the common stock should be used to describe God is not surprising. Newly independent countries take over the names "Prime Minister" and "Parliament" for their own use, but the names may have different implications from what they have in this country. Or it may happen that the thing changes but the name remains the same. The word "battleship" meant something very different by the time of Admiral Sir Dudley Pound from what it had meant (in the longer form "line-of-battle ship") in the time of Nelson. That the gods of various peoples in the Near East had etymologically similar names may mean that the original conception of a god had been unwittingly spread throughout the ancient world, or it may mean that only the name had been spread. New recruits asked for their religion for purposes of identification may all reply "Church of England" but probably each of them will have his own understanding of what he means. Out of the grunts of Stone Age men there presumably arose, long before writing was thought of, a limited agreed vocabulary relating to food, drink, life, death, sex and fighting. Religious terminology developed out of this rudimentary vocabulary and was, one supposes, developed in distinctive ways by various groups. It would certainly not be at odds with orthodox belief to understand, as Mr Allegro seems to suggest, that the peoples of the Near East gained a common language with a commonly accepted name for the supreme being. It is no difficulty to believe that, this being the case, one of those peoples should be favoured with a special revelation from God and should retain, and later write down, the proclamations and undertakings made to them alone of all peoples. If God decided to speak to human beings he would speak to them in words they would understand.

All-pervasive and inescapable, sexual themes are found in every department of life, more or less consciously present in the minds of all. It is not surprising that man's religious vocabulary should be heavily impregnated (saving the word) with sexual terms. His knowledge of sex was prior to his knowledge of God; the revelation of himself which God made to his creatures after the Fall was a revelation which necessarily had to be expressed in terms of an existing vocabulary. It is not part of Christian belief to accept that God had to teach human beings a new language before he could speak to them. If the names of God had a close connexion with the life-giving terms already appropriated for sexual fecundity, then these were names which asserted the Creator's claim over all aspects of his creation.

There is in short no good reason for thinking that God should need to invent a new language when he wanted to speak to man, nor that man should need to learn that new language. If God spoke to man at all, it is reasonable to believe that he spoke to him where he was and in terms that he could understand. If man's language from the beginning was weighted with sexual content, that sexual content would not be eliminated by virtue of the fact that the message being received was a religious one. Those who favour the *Daily Mirror* before they become Christians do not automatically switch to the *Guardian*, or even the *Telegraph*, as a result of their conversion! But the important proviso is: "If God spoke to men at all ..." Throughout Mr Allegro's book is the assumption that God, if he exists at all, does not speak to man; religion is just not that kind of thing.

Mr Allegro assembles an etymological array sufficient to bring a gasp of admiration from any man. Even the non-specialist can understand something of the significance of Mr Allegro's daring exploration of unknown linguistic territory. The possibility of accurately relating the Indo-European

93

and Semitic groups of languages to each other could well lead to the revision of a good many accepted ideas. The names Zeus and Yahweh, says Mr Allegro, are both derived from a Sumerian original meaning spermatozoa. The names Dionysus (i.e. Bacchus) and Jesus similarly have a common Sumerian original, meaning "seed that saves". The early part of Mr Allegro's book is characterised by an abounding confidence that a new linguistic age has dawned. "For the first time, it becomes possible to decipher the names of gods, mythological characters, classical and biblical, and plant names." "At long last identification of the main characters of many of the old classical and biblical mythologies is possible, since we can now decipher their names." (p. xviii) "The dramatic step forward that is now possible in our researches into the origin of Near Eastern cults and mythologies arises from our ability to make these decipherments. We can now break down god-names like Zeus and Yahweh/Jehovah, and hero-names like Dionysus and Jesus, because it is possible to penetrate the linguistic barriers imposed by the different languages in which their respective literatures have reached us." (p.6)

A certain amount of jubilation is in order when an outstandingly difficult code has been cracked, but one cannot avoid the conclusion that Mr Allegro has allowed his zeal to run away with him. Exuberant repetition drives the main point firmly home, but we have to remember the speculative nature of many of Mr Allegro's verbal reconstructions (to which he himself draws attention on page 16 of his book). Like Lord Randolph Churchill's "damned dots", the asterisks found frequently in Mr Allegro's book may be daunting, but their indication of a purely speculative verbal group must not be allowed to escape the reader. Mr Allegro's linguistic conclusions are necessarily tentative rather than conclusive, as he himself acknowledges. When considering the more startling of Mr Allegro's assertions, the reader is well advised to turn repeatedly to the careful qualifications which he makes about the basis upon which his assertions rest.

To find words from one language appearing in another is no uncommon experience. In the fourteenth century in this country, for example, Chaucer used a great many words of French origin and the influx of words from across the Channel changed the character of the language a good deal, but nobody would say that because of this the English language may be regarded as a development of French. The connection between Middle English and Old English makes the true origin of English clear, however many loan-words may have been introduced into it. What is true of the relationship between English and French is even more true of the relationship between Hebrew and Sumerian, because Hebrew and Sumerian are further apart to start with. Something more than a collection of loan-words is necessary before any clear relationship is demonstrated between Sumerian and other languages. Yet Mr Allegro makes unwarranted claims in this field without providing anything more substantial. This at least is the view taken by philologists.

The basic phoneme "U" with which Mr Allegro deals on page 20 is fundamental to the question. YA-U means, so Mr Allegro tells us, "juice of fertility". (It is also echoed, interestingly enough, in the name Swift makes his intellectual horses give to the depraved human creatures whom they despise, the Yahoos; perhaps here we have an atavistic verbal form that broke through to the conscious mind of the unhappy Dean and that can now be seen as conveying another overtone to the misanthropic appellation.) Like the mushroom itself, Mr Allegro's book is full of juice, but the reader of *The Sacred Mushroom and the Cross* will find himself obliged to ask whether on Mr Allegro's own showing the two phonemes YA and U when put together may not equally well mean "strong water of vegetation" or "strong water of rain" or "strong water of the storm-god". It may be true that the early Sumerian regarded rain as heavenly semen. It may be true that on this understanding certain plants would have been regarded as being better endowed with the god's semen than other plants. There are, however, other possible explanations, and these have to be considered before Mr Allegro's choice of explanation is accepted.

Mr Allegro's multi-lingual punning, his plethora of recondite allusions, his urbane trafficking in literary jokes makes the New Testament an altogether different matter from what we have in our innocence traditionally taken it to be. We have to read the New Testament not to discover its ostensible meaning but with an eye open for previously undiscovered puns. No longer can we say that the Bible is a book that the simplest can profit from as well as the most erudite. The Bible must on Mr Allegro's view be handed over to the specialists, for it is only the man with a working knowledge of Sumerian philology who can make the intended meaning of the Bible – or at least of the New Testament – plain.

Mushrooms and mandrakes

We have now at least the advantage of knowing the most ancient language of the area and can in many cases begin to decipher the names of the plants and their attendant angels and demons. But it has to be recognised that of all the branches of research into the life of the ancient world, identification of plant names is one of the most difficult.

John M. Allegro, *The Sacred Mushroom and the Cross*

To understand Mr Allegro's interpretation of the New Testament we have to forget that we ever heard of aspirin. We also have to forget hypodermic syringes, electro-cardiograms and pace-makers. We have to take ourselves back to the days before readily available pills with the precise formula printed on the label. We have to take ourselves back to the days described by Flora Thompson in *Lark Rise to Candleford* when every woman in the village had a herb corner in the garden, when rue, camomile, peppermint, pennyroyal and horehound were all used for one medicinal purpose or another. We have to take ourselves back to the days when Parson Woodforde's maid Lizzy had bark (i.e. quinine) prescribed for her by an eighteenth century doctor. Lizzy's trouble was probably caused more by a disagreeable suitor than by anything else, but bark was a favourite remedy of Woodforde's doctor, and if it proved too effective a purge it could be followed by laudanum. A draught of rhubarb was another favourite remedy, and Woodforde had his own stand-bys – "the second ring of Alder stick steeped in water" for example.

Today the very names of these medicinal plants are fading from consciousness. Digitalis replaces foxglove, morphine replaces laudanum. Precisely measured doses replace the by guess and by God methods that used to prevail. But if we are to understand the enormous significance of the multitudinous plants known to have unexpected potencies, we must attempt to put ourselves into the position of those who could not call at the

99

chemist's when they had headache or indigestion but had to go out into the garden to pull up a weed. We do well to remind ourselves that until quite recently it was customary to find men behind market-stalls selling their own potions and pastes which, they said, had been used with benefit by many of the crowned heads of Europe. A formula was the last thing one would find on the label in such a case; once the stall-holder divulged his catch-penny secret recipe his livelihood was gone. But apart from the quacks and their placebos there were the familiar country remedies that had to serve Flora Thompson, Parson Woodforde and all the generations back to Noah during the days when medicine struggled to free itself from the astrologer and the barber. Until the middle of the nineteenth century crude vegetable extracts and inorganic compounds were all that was available in the way of a pharmacopoeia. Outlandish animal extracts found their way into the mixtures prepared by medical practitioners on the fringe as they found their way into the witches' cauldron in *Macbeth*, but in general the available drugs were to be found first in the hedgerow and then, more expensively, in the apothecary's shop. Senna pods, laudanum and quinine were exotic additions to the vegetable armoury of the medical practitioner.

In the pre-penicillin days of tinctures and powders, of berries and roots, plants of unusual potency were likely to be credited with supernatural capabilities. Umbriel, "a dusky, melancholy sprite",who set off for the Cave of Spleen after Belinda had lost her lock of hair in Alexander Pope's *Rape of the Lock*, faced fiends and spectres on the journey, but

> Safe passed the gnome through this fantastic band,
> A branch of healing spleenwort in his hand.

In safeguarding himself in this way he was doing no more than Odysseus had done when he protected himself with a herb called moly against the enchantments of Circe, who had already changed his companions into pigs. In *Comus* John Milton refers to "a small unsightly root, but of divine effect" called haemony. More medicinal than moly, it protected a man against enchantments, mildew blast, damp "or gastly furies apparition".

Mandrakes were commonly alluded to in Elizabethan literature; their appearance and the belief that they cried out when pulled from the ground provided readily understood allusions in an age which was neither furtive or squeamish. "Get with child a mandrake roote" wrote John Donne, referring to the bifurcated manlike, or womanlike, shape of its root. Shakespeare's Juliet talks of "shrieks like mandrakes' torn out of the earth" and his Iago says:

Not poppy, nor mandragora,

Nor all the drowsy syrups of the world,

Shall ever medicine thee to that sweet sleep

Which thou owedst yesterday..

The mandrake (or mandragora) enjoyed a reputation as a narcotic; it was also famed as an aphrodisiac, as we see from Genesis 30.

Similar to the mandrake as a plant with a distinctive reputation was the medlar. Its appearance was suggestive and it was eaten when decayed. Hence Lucio in *Measure for Measure* could refer to the girl he had seduced as a rotten medlar. Mercutio in *Romeo and Juliet* could compare a willing girl with a medlar. The fig was a similarly significant fruit.

If mandrake was an aphrodisiac, so were many other plants—at least in popular estimation. Red pepper, belladonna, Indian hemp, camphor and cantharidin have all with good reason or otherwise been esteemed as heightening sexual desire. A few plants — wormseed, for example — were believed to have the opposite effect.

From the earliest times men looked amongst the plants around them for medicinal agents. They were never short of possibilities. Berries, roots, rinds and pulp provided endless permutations offering hope to those who had so far found no cure for their ailment. Always there was the possibility that some strange new plant would provide a potion or a powder that would take away the blotches or ease the heartburn or improve the hearing. It is against this background that we must consider the fly agaric, a background of homely and imprecise medical preparations, a background of folklore and guesswork, a background in which the terminology varied from one county to another.

Mr Allegro's theory requires us to ignore the vast bulk of the age-old rustic pharmacopoeia and concentrate our gaze on one group – the fungi. And of the fifty thousand species in this group, we must select the ten thousand members of the mushroom family. And of these ten thousand only one, the fly agaric or *amanita muscaria*, must have our undivided attention, for only this solitary type is of incomparable worth. We shall readily agree that many other members of the fungus family are patently worthless. Dry-rot is a fungus we are glad to see the back of; its mycelium weft reaching silently into fresh territory and reducing sound timber to a cracked and brittle skin makes it a malevolent enemy of mankind. We shall have to concede that the saphrophytes, unpleasant as they seem, perform a useful service by causing decay and by converting dead plants into something better. More evidently beneficial is the common mould, *penicillin notatus*, which has given man an invaluable antibiotic. Amateurs of the fungi will perhaps be able to extend the list of fungi that are beneficial as well as interesting to mankind. But interest must be concentrated. The array of mushrooms of differing shapes and sizes containing varied mixtures of alkaloids, must yield pride of place to the fly agaric. It is the fly agaric above all other plants on the face of the earth that demands the attention of the man who is looking into the religious history of mankind.

The henbane, the horse-radish, and the hop, mint, mustard and mulberry, shamrock, sorrel and sundew must all yield place to this gaudy fungus. Its shape, its colour, its properties make it the king of the plants — as indeed the biblical fable found in Judges 9 suggests, according to Mr Allegro. The olive, the fig and the vine — each well deserving, one might have thought, a place in the sun — had to yield first place to the lowly mushroom; for Mr Allegro assures us that what we have always understood to be a mere bramble — an unflattering description of Abimelech compared with the people who were making a worthwhile contribution to the life of the nation — we must now understand to be the fly agaric. Here, says Mr Allegro, is a piece of vegetation mythology marooned at this point in the Bible for no good reason and originally intended to show the worth of the mighty mushroom. We must make a choice; we can retain the traditional interpretation and place the supplanter Abimelech along with the worthless bramble low down on the scale beneath the olive, fig and vine, or we can applaud the mushroom as the neglected and despised possessor of a great secret and advance it to chief place among the plants.

One thing we must ask ourselves is this: has Mr Allegro provided sufficient evidence of identification as far as the fly agaric is concerned? When he draws our attention to the numerous references in ancient writers to potent plants, is he correct in claiming that the writers were intending, in those instances which he cites, to refer to the fly agaric? On the face of it the writers concerned were referring to many different plants, to hellebore, paeony and chicory amongst others. We have to decide whether Mr Allegro has managed to bring order out of confusion or whether he has imposed on the ancient writers an order which is entirely of his own making, determined more by the requirements of his theory than by an objective assessment of the evidence.

Identification of plant names is one of the most difficult

branches of research into the life of the ancient world, says Mr Allegro, and this has to be borne in mind by the reader following his argument about the properties of the fly agaric. Many different popular names are given to the same plant, particularly in the case of the more noteworthy plants, and this makes it difficult to determine which plant is indicated at any particular point. "Even now," writes Mr Allegro (page 36), "the inexactitude of local plant names is the despair of field botanists." One can only applaud Mr Allegro's candour and call to mind the pernicious weed which in England is called ground elder but in Presbyterian Scotland is called bishopweed; the same plant is also named bishop's elder, goutweed or herb gerard. The "gerard" part is derived from the saint who looked after the cellar at Clairvaux and needed a cure for gout. One remembers also how the names "bryony", "hemlock" and "violet" have been applied to various plants.

On page 37 of his book Mr Allegro concludes that the plant described by Pliny as a paeony cannot possibly be the paeony we know; and most readers would agree, for Pliny's plant bore on the top of its stem four or five growths like almonds which contained a large amount of red and black seed. But most readers are unlikely to conclude that this description fits the fly agaric, even though on etymological grounds Mr Allegro argues that Pliny's paeony was in fact a fly agaric.

Sumerian, it is said, provides the answer to a mystery presented by one of the names given by Pliny to the paeony. The name is *Glycyside*. Meaningless in Latin or Greek, this term is said by Mr Allegro to be a jumbled form of an old Sumerian plant-name meaning "bolt-gourd" or "mushroom".

The mandrake, claims Mr Allegro, can be identified as the mushroom. This will surprise the reader who understood the mandrake to belong to the same family as the tobacco, the petunia and the potato. The mandrake, argues Mr Allegro, is to be identified with the fly agaric because one of the Greek names of the mandrake, *antimimon*, is traceable to a Sumerian original meaning "heavenly shade". The etymology of "mandrake" or "mandragora" leads the inquirer, so we are told, to a hypothetical Sumerian form meaning "demon or fate-plant of the field". Mr Allegro concludes that this hypothetical form is also the origin of the word "nectar", the food of the gods.

Pliny's description of the taking of hellebore is probably, says Mr Allegro, a description of the taking of the mushroom. The alarming symptoms described by Pliny – sneezing, vomiting – are what one might expect after taking a plant containing muscarine, atropine and bufotenin, argues Mr Allegro.

The assassins did not, as has been commonly supposed, resort to cannabis resin to nerve them for their murderous tasks; no, says Mr Allegro, they were addicted to the fly agaric. The Greek word *kannabis* is derived, says Mr Allegro, from the Sumerian element GAN meaning mushroom top. To this is added the second part of the name "Barnabas" meaning "red, speckled with white".

Sumerian verbal roots applied to the mushroom are also applied to other plants. The crocus is mentioned by Mr Allegro as one example, the phallic form of its stem and flower being the reason for this. Mr Allegro does not, however, conclude that the crocus had a place in the mushroom cult; nor does he conclude that the crocus was actually a mushroom.

Pliny's description of chicory leaves no doubt that the plant he is describing is not the plant we know by that name. Pliny speaks of people anointing themselves with the juice of the plant. Mr Allegro therefore goes on to conclude that this plant is none other than the mandrake – i.e. the mushroom mandrake, not the mandrake which we know. Very common in the phallic nomenclature of mushrooms, says Mr Allegro, is a Sumerian root meaning the crown of the penis. This word is also applied to the plant asparagus which, far from being an aphrodisiac mushroom is an anaphrodisiac green plant.

The reader may be pardoned for declaring himself not altogether convinced by Mr Allegro's arguments. The supreme place of the fly agaric must rest upon something better than hypothetical word-forms and speculative identification of the actual plants.

Another dubious matter is the question of whether the *amanita muscaria* has ever grown in or around Palestine. If the mushroom cult could only flourish by virtue of supplies brought from afar the improbability of the cult's existence is greatly increased. The point is worth emphasising, for it is a particular example of the general principle that it is Mr Allegro who must provide positive evidence to support his theory. It is he who is proposing extraordinary explanations of matters already accounted for otherwise; it is he therefore who must offer substantial support at every possible point if he is to persuade readers to abandon views already held. The absence of positive evidence about the *amanita muscaria* being indigenous to the country where it is said to have assumed such importance' is a serious weakness in Mr Allegro's case.

We can only conclude that in the vast and confused array of plant lore there is not sufficient evidence to show that the fly agaric is the original source of the numerous tales and legends mistakenly (as Mr Allegro alleges) attached to the paeony, the mandrake, the hellebore and the chicory as well as to the fly agaric itself. Mr Allegro may be right in attributing to the fly agaric descriptions attributed by the originators of the descriptions to other plants altogether, but we do not know. Alkaloids of one kind and another are found abundantly in numerous plants. We do not know that the fly agaric has ever grown in the region where the mushroom cult is said by Mr Allegro to have flourished. In view of these factors cautious scepticism is the most appropriate attitude to Mr Allegro's botanical assertions.

Cunning myth-makers

There is every reason why there should *not* have been a real Jesus of Nazareth, at least not one connected with the sect of Christians, nor a real John the Baptist, Peter, John, James, and so on.

John M. Allegro, *The Sacred Mushroom and the Cross*

Mr Allegro is not the first to suggest that the Christian religion is founded upon a fiction, that Jesus never lived. Roderick Dunkerley, in his Pelican *Beyond the Gospels* mentions J.M. Robertson, Arthur Drews and P.L. Couchoud as "chief exponents of this fantastic notion" and quotes Sir James Frazer, author of *The Golden Bough*, as saying: "The doubts which have been cast on the historical reality of Jesus are in my judgment unworthy of serious attention." Of course, to investigate references to Jesus outside the New Testament is, on the terms proposed by Mr Allegro, to do no more than cite works produced by men who were themselves either deceived by or party to the "Christian" conspiracy, but the number of references dealt with by Dr Dunkerley in his book increases the weight of probability in favour of an orthodox understanding of Jesus as a historical person because it is evidence of the widespread impact made by a remarkable religious teacher. Discussing the idea of Jesus as being the mythical embodiment of a new departure in mystery religions, Professor C.H. Dodd allows that such a theory is based on well-recognised facts. "But," he continues, "in order to show that the Christian religion was no more than an offshoot of some Hellenistic cult, the advocates of the theory need to make a whole series of completely unverifiable assumptions. The contrary view, that the emergence of the Christian religion was the direct result of a series of historical events which took place in Palestine under the governorship of Pontius Pilate, is one which needs the

109

fewest unverifiable hypotheses; and it has the merit that it accords with the view taken of Christian origins both by all our earliest Christian documents, and also in the earliest non-Christian sources, such as they are." (*History and the Gospel*, Hodder and Stoughton)

Mr Allegro in effect claims to have produced material which puts the "whole series of completely unverifiable assumptions" referred to by Professor Dodd in a new light. It may indeed be the case that the series of assumptions is slightly shorter, but other improbabilities have been introduced.

If we accept the view that the New Testament was compiled by mushroom worshippers in order to divert attention from their own activities, what was the extent of their achievement? To gauge this, it is necessary to remind oneself of the immense amount of work that has been done on Gospel sources, for example, by scholars anxious to discover how and why the Gospels came to be put together. On the face of it the Gospels are straightforward accounts of the life and death (with an undue amount of space given to the death) of Jesus. To the most casual reader the fourth Gospel appears different from the other three, but the first three obviously have a great deal in common. Closer examination, however, reveals that there are blocks of material which are repeated in all three. Most of Mark appears in Matthew and Luke, and Matthew and Luke also have a large number of verses in common which do not occur in Mark. This has led scholars to conclude that the writers of Matthew and Luke incorporated into their account a collection of material already in existence and known as Q, and the material forming the Gospel according to Mark. Basically, then, the material in the first three Gospels can be broken up into blocks and assigned to different sources. When we consider the distinctive elements in Luke, shall we say, we see that to the basic material (Mark and Q) has been added other material – birth narratives, for example – which does not occur

110

in other Gospels. The slant of Luke's Gospel, its preservation of parables which are not found in the other Gospels, its accent on prayer, its attention to the women who met Jesus, all these things give the Gospel a distinctive flavour with the result that one can almost see the writer before one — a cultured, travelled man, a man who had taken the trouble to collect stories about Jesus from sources in Judaea, a man who was writing his Gospel to show the breadth of Jesus' outlook and to commend him to a friend who appears to have occupied an influential position. The impression made on the man who sits down to read through first Mark's Gospel, then Luke's is that of two quite differing points of view. Mark's Gospel seems sharp, urgent, almost breathless; Luke's is more measured, more elegant, more impressive as a piece of craftsmanship. When we move on to consider the distinctive features of Matthew's Gospel — carefully arranged blocks of teaching, the importance attached to the fulfilment of Old Testament prophecy, for example — we see that this Gospel drew on material unknown to Luke and was written with a different readership in mind; it was written for the Jews. The fourth Gospel is different again; indeed, it stands in a class by itself. Whereas in the first three Gospels (and particularly in Mark) Jesus seems almost terse; in the fourth Gospel Jesus seems almost long-winded. Plainly the material has been modified as we might expect to be the case when an old man was compiling his account after living with and reflecting upon the story for many years.

These characteristics have been discovered and minutely examined by scholars until they are able to draw up a complicated chart (as in Dr F.C. Grant's *The Gospels — their origin and their growth*, Faber) showing numerous distinctive sources which can with varying degrees of assurance be traced in the Gospels as we now know them. In fact, it appears that a large number of people contributed to the final form of the

Gospels — by their recollections, by the passing on of traditional teaching, by editorial work at the final stage. Whereas the four Gospels with their varying emphases had always seemed to have a rough-hewn authenticity that showed they had obviously not been elaborately reconciled with one another, the conception of a considerable number of pre-existing elements finding their way into the finished form of the Gospels gives this uncontrived note of authenticity further confirmation. The more complex we see the compilation of the Gospels to have been, the more trustworthy it makes them.

Now to suppose that the Gospels were given their far from simple characteristics by a man or a group of men who were concerned to do no more than lead others astray and at the same time to conceal the name of their most precious cultic object, the fly agaric, as frequently as possible in the finished product, is breath-taking. The perpetrators of this blind or hoax put into their work a degree of subtlety which can never have been equalled. Not only did they compose two entirely different documents covering different aspects of this imaginary person Jesus. They then presented the two documents to one man and told him to combine the two and fill out his composition with stories made up by his acquaintances so as to make the whole thing appear to be directed to winning over non-Jews to this new movement. When he had finished his job, the two documents he had been working from were handed to another man who was told to combine the two and fill out his composition so as to present as good a case as possible to the Jews. When this had been done, the first of the new compositions was called the Gospel according to St Luke, the second the Gospel according to St Matthew. Of the original two documents one was kept and named the Gospel according to St Mark; the other was lost or destroyed. Although such elaborate care as this was taken in the composition of documents intended to be no more than a blind, no attempt was made to reconcile the varying accounts so as to eliminate points that would obviously confuse the reader. To complete the collection of Gospels another man was invited to imagine he was writing long after the events described and to frame his account after the style of an old man. This man's composition was called the Gospel according to St. John.

A performance like this argues a measure of literary astuteness, imaginative ingenuity and Machiavellian cunning that can never have been surpassed. Compared with this, the forging of bank-notes is child's play. The mushroom worshippers did a job not merely good enough to fool the Roman and Jewish authorities who were making life uncomfortable for them; they did a job good enough to fool generation after generation of linguistic scholars, source-seekers, form-critics. The far-sightedness, incomparable thoroughness and the sure touch of these men can never have been equalled. The mind boggles at such a performance. Yet such a performance as this we must accept if Mr Allegro's theory is correct.

Having recognised the artfulness of these cunning myth-makers, we have to acknowledge another aspect of their character. Like many creative workers, they were lamentably absent-minded. Deft as they were in threading puns to make a glittering string, inventive as they were in elaborating their basic plot, perceptive as they were in creating true-to-life characters, they were singularly forgetful about including information of the highest importance to their readers. There is more than a glimpse of human comedy in the notion of these first century writers lovingly pouring out their imaginative talent and becoming so engrossed in their creation that they forgot to include the very details which the composition was originally designed to bear. Carried away by their poetic fervour, they developed their literary masterpiece with no regard for its practical purpose; enchanted by the new creation they were bringing to birth, they allowed themselves to fall under its spell. Instead of the practical guide which they (or their masters) had originally desired, they allowed themselves to produce a bewitching story which engaged their whole attention so that their original intention was quite overlooked.

The incantations and rites, the bodily and mental preparations, the carefully preserved observations of centuries – these were the secrets which, on Mr Allegro's view, were essential to the activities of the mushroom cult and which were reluctantly but under a sense of necessity committed to writing during the Jewish Revolt which ended in the destruction of Jerusalem in AD 70. But when we examine the coded material embedded in the New Testament we find no details to enable a man to enjoy the benefits of the fly agaric. All we find is re-iteration of the name of the plant and one or two incantations. Brave would he be who approached the fearful plant armed only with this information! He might find himself taking an enormous overdose which would throw his body into convulsions, paralyse him and then carry him off in a confusion of hallucinations and flashing lights to an agonising death. Far from knowing the main features of the cult, we know only the name of the cultic plant, its appearance, and the incantation to be used when plucking it out of the ground. The practical details of the cult have not been set down for our enlightenment. The message-hiders were very slow to foresee what information would actually be needed. Ingenious as they were to invent a story about Jesus the Messiah, they omitted to include such matters as dosage levels in their cabalistic compositions.

What pedestrian cryptographers the mushroom worshippers were! They went to endless trouble to fabricate stories about a non-existent Saviour; they invented numerous episodes to add to the credibility of their invention, even though those episodes added nothing to the composition from their own point of view They left false clues to put scholars off their track – so successfully that nineteen centuries later the false clues are still being taken seriously. They invented a mysterious personage of such originality and credibility that he exacted obedience from many subsequent generations. They did all these things in order to pass on their secret to those who might deserve to find it. And now that Mr Allegro has shown us these things, what is their secret? What is it that is carefully hidden in the Bible so that only a student of Sumerian philology can reveal it? Is it a list of requirements of those who would approach the central mystery? Are the appropriate dosages set out for the benefit of later generations? Do we find advice about whether this most potent fungus should be swallowed, sniffed or drunk after being dissolved in wine? Is there a description of the effects of the drug, including a warning about after-effects? Is there any indication that the fly agaric contains a drug of addiction? Are there any remedies for an overdose or for those allergic to agaric? There are none of these things. All we have after "breaking the code" is a succession of variations on the name of a fungus and a few incantations. We have to ask whether it was worthwhile going to all that trouble merely to pass on a name, important though knowledge of a name was held to be. As for the incantations, a generation that is familiar with the slogans chanted by football supporters cannot smile in all that superior a fashion about slogans chanted in the course of a religious rite, but were the incantations worth all that bother? What waste of literary talent! What prodigality of misdirected inventiveness! Never in the field of religious history was so much word-play made by so many to convey so little. And to what end? Only to draw other men's attention to a potent fertility symbol and to suggest that provided care is taken in the gathering of it, it is a good idea to eat the sacred mushroom to the greater glory of fecundity.

One further thing must be said at this point. There is a minatory tone about Mr Allegro's insistence that if only one of the mushroom references he claims to have discovered is correct then an intention to deceive is indicated. At this point he protests too much. To base a reassessment of the New Testament on a few presumptive puns is to build on a dangerously inadequate foundation. If we reassessed that arch-punner Shakespeare in such a way we should invite amused smiles. If the vital pun about the sons of thunder is to bear such weight, it must be shown conclusively that the pun was calculated, intelligible to potential readers and incomprehensible to the Roman authorities. This is to suppose that the mushroom cult forgers were adept in etymology and that the putative recipients of their secrets were equally alert to verbal echoes and half-veiled allusions. It is also to suppose that the Roman authorities were no more than buffoons when it came to a matter of examining the documents of a troublesome religious sect for mischievous material. Capable and educated as the mushroom cult leaders may have been, they increasingly emerge as giants among men on Mr Allegro's reading of the situation. Master forgers, adroit etymologists, daring tweakers of the imperial nose as it sniffed out sedition; what men they were! Whatever acts of savagery they may conceivably have perpetrated when under the influence of their diminutive god, they did not do things by halves when elaborate evasive tactics were required. If such men were alive today they could state their preference and name their price in the matter of selling their services. Counter-intelligence, advertising copywriting, coding work, script-writing — they would find the world at their feet.

What a lame tale! What an empty vessel clanging away its repetitious and empty story! Truly the mountains have travailed and brought forth a mouse. Truly, whatever the mushroom cult set out to achieve by composing the New Testament, they have shown themselves the greatest hoaxers in history. As a result of their efforts men have poured out their energies without stint; they have performed heroic deeds; they have accomplished brilliant feats of intellect; they have surprised themselves and others and transformed the face of the world. Yet all the time they were mistaken. What they should have done, if only they could have got the message straight, was to sit down and eat the mushroom. Poor wretched Christians! All they have suffered and all they have achieved has been suffered and achieved in the service of an illusion. Can anything in human history be sadder than this, that for the sake of a Saviour who never existed and for the sake of a god who is unknown men have invented dreams which have not given easy consolation but have called out every ounce of their strength and ability? Alas, what boots it? Better to eat lotus and simulate heaven than pray and sweat for a kingdom without a King.

What else had these arch-deceivers to do in order to put about the story that far from indulging in alkaloids and phallic symbols they were innocently, indeed virtuously attempting to follow the teachings of a young rabbi who had unfortunately been executed by the Romans? We cannot be clear about this. Mr Allegro suggests that the cover story was designed to afford protection from both Romans and Jews, yet the story they compiled was a story calculated to outrage the sensibilities of the Jewish leaders, high priests and Pharisees alike, and to alienate the moderate, let alone the irascible element in ortho-- dox Judaism. Perhaps once they had got away from the immediate objective they had in mind, the smuggling in of bits and pieces of cultic information, their interest waned and the rest of what we know as the New Testament degenerated into a piece of pot-boiling. Perhaps the job of plodding through the doctrinal sections of the Epistles was left to an apprentice who had a private passion for theological speculation. Or perhaps there is a great deal in the New Testament that records not the story that the mushroom cult wished to see preserved but the record of the parallel movement, Christianity that we should now recognise as orthodox, with no subterranean meaning to it at all. Orthodox Christianity, remember, was the villain of the piece at this time; it was deeply opposed to the mushroom cult and anxious to stamp it out. Perhaps one of the first victims in the stamping out process was the mushroom story. Perhaps all we have is a collection of mutilated documents that neither mushroom worshippers nor orthodox Christians would approve.

To embark upon such speculation is to see an unfathomable gulf opening up at one's feet. Who wrote what? Where do mushroom writers end and orthodox Christian writers take over? Was it the mushroom worshippers or the Christians who composed I Corinthians 13? If it was the former, with what motive did they compose it — to lay a false trail, to make themselves appear virtuous, because they genuinely loved love? We ponder in vain. Clarity and certainty are on the further side of the gulf and there is no means of crossing. Able and enterprising as the arch-deceivers were, they could not guarantee the safe survival of their compositions in their original purity. Perhaps other hands sullied the impeccable allegorical guides to the mushroom cult. Perhaps the wicked Christians or the vindictive Jews tampered with the mushroom masterpieces. We do not know. When we have accepted Mr Allegro's findings and acknowledged the existence of the mushroom worshippers we have traded in an understanding of the New Testament that is full of difficulties but reasonable for one that is so muddled and incomprehensible as to drive a man to drink or to fly agaric. Ah, perhaps that was the intention! Those magnificent men were capable of a subtlety as great as that. They were capable of anything.

Hapless alchemists

Mr Allegro compels us to rewrite our history books. On the day that his views are accepted by a substantial weight of informed opinion we shall all have to make fresh assessments of the cardinal figures of history. Those outstanding men whom we have been accustomed to regard as intellectual pioneers and champions of religious liberty will now have to be down-graded. A sober post-Allegro estimation will regard them as deluded men determined to see the rest of mankind as deeply bogged down as themselves. The contingent who set sail for the New World in the *Mayflower*, the poet John Milton, Dr Arnold of Rugby, Sir Thomas More were all great but misguided men who sought in their own way to bring fresh territories under the reign of a non-existent Christ. If only they had realised it, they were spending their lives in the service of a fiction. A new nation (later to prove the greatest the world has ever seen), the only epic of any importance in modern English, the archetype of English public schools, the championing of integrity in the face of a despotic monarch — all these achievements were inspired by a misunderstanding of a designedly deceptive document.

The nature of the fresh assessment that will be required is overwhelming. The work will be enough to keep scholars busy for generations. But there is one group of men whose lustre will not be dimmed by post-Allegro scholarship; indeed, in all probability it will appear that these men remained true to what glimmer of truth remained in the world after the early Christians had stamped out opposing schools of thought. The group in question comprises the alchemists. When the true light had all but vanished from the earth to be succeeded by the gross darkness of the Christian era, these single-minded men persisted in their belief that there were secrets about the universe to be discovered outside the docile communities of scholars set up by the Church. When religion dominated centres of learning and prescribed boundaries that would curb speculation, a small group of men insisted on seeking out knowledge above and beyond that authorised by the Pope and the Bible. Regarded with varying degrees of approval, these men with their independent ways and clear objectives reminded every generation that passed their murky doorways that the Christian faith did not provide all that a man needed to know about the ultimate mysteries of the universe. The alchemists were in the Great Tradition, a tradition overlaid by the Christians, kept alive by alchemists, quacks and herb-chewing rustics and blossoming today in the LSD and mescalin cults. It is as faithful supporters of the Great Tradition that the alchemists must be reconsidered.

The despised and unorthodox alchemists worked unceasingly to discover two secrets. One was the philosopher's stone which would enable them to turn base metals into gold; the other was the elixir of life which would enable them to prolong life indefinitely. The former quest was plainly inspired by a desire for a direct route to power; but as for the elixir of life, is it not reasonable to regard this as coming in direct line of descent from the mushroom sect? Were not the alchemists in fact pursuing without the aid of the information concealed in the New Testament a corrupted version of the goal previously attained by the devotees of the *amanita muscaria*?

We shall have to be ready to wipe off our faces any trace of condescension when we consider the alchemists. Post-Allegro scholarship may well show us that these ever-hopeful men working among their retorts, with fumes discolouring the ceiling, with the furnace making them sweat, with their assistants keeping a sharp eye open for any sign of success, and with their undeniably impressive jargon – putrefaction, solution, ablution, sublimation, cohobation, calcination, ceration, fixation, mortification, vivification – daunting the sceptical inquirer, were nearer the truth than we thought. As they persisted in the belief that all metals were variations on the same basic material, and that the right tincture would enable them to bring about the astounding feat of transmutation as well as healing diseases and prolonging life, they were, although they did not know it, labouring to rediscover the more modest but more feasible secret contained in the fly agaric. As they went on searching for the key to power and immortality, scarcely noticing that they were growing older, encouraged to continue by wealthy customers prepared to pay for by-products, encouraged all too often, alas, by gullible admirers who were too ready to part with their cash, the alchemists are not pitiable figures whom we can afford to ignore; they represent, however unsatisfactory their methods, a continuing tradition, a tradition that may go back to the days of the persecuted mushroom cult.

If only medieval alchemists had picked up even a hint of the secret contained in the fly agaric, they might have astonished the world. They could have confounded the sceptics, vindicated their own distinctive faith and brought at least a foretaste of everlasting bliss to their fellow-men. The power that they sought by an abundance of gold would have been theirs as they sold phials of mushroom juice at an exorbitant price. The immortality that they hoped to enjoy would be sampled as men rose to heights of ecstasy otherwise unattainable under the influence of carefully measured doses of fly agaric alkaloids. But right as the alchemists were in seeking out their two objectives, they were wrong in their understanding of their actual form. They mixed, heated, distilled and infused when they should have been out under the pine trees plucking and licking mushrooms. They thought that the secrets they sought could be discovered by working with alembics, filters and bolt's-heads when they could only be discovered by fieldwork. Instead of seeking out an impossible elixir, they might have accepted as no mean substitute a drug to heighten their perceptions and renew their fading capacity for sexual enjoyment. But they could not do this; they lacked the secret. So successful had the mushroom cult been in throwing their persecutors off the track that the central feature of their fertility cult had been entirely overlaid. Little did the alchemists know that what they were desperately seeking to discover had already been discovered and forgotten over a thousand years before. In the light of Mr Allegro's revelations the alchemists become the saddest men of history, seeking by infusion and distillation what could be recovered in the event only by philology, looking for a stone when they should have been looking for a mushroom, hoping to manufacture gold which would give them power to indulge their desires when all the time the indulgence of those desires could be obtained directly by plucking a plant growing in their own back gardens.

The discoveries that these unhappy men made by accident in the course of their alchemy are forgotten; we forget these examples of serendipity — gunpowder, Dresden porcelain, Glauber's salts — and pity pathetic men persuading themselves after every failure that success was just around the corner, that one day the equivalent of Aladdin's ring, the balsam of Ferabras and Prince Ahmed's apple would come to light. Ben Jonson's play *The Alchemist* acquires new overtones of irony when the failure of these men to turn to the ancient fertility religions for their elixir is remembered. Particularly ironic is it when we recall that according to Jonson the alchemists, like the mushroom worshippers, found traces and hints of their secrets in the ancient world and its mythology – in Jason's fleece, Jove's shower, and even in a treatise concerning the philosopher's stone, written by Adam in High Dutch ("the primitive tongue") on cedar board. Even in their own laboratories the alchemists could have found pointers to the mushroom – a bolt's-head (blushing as it became ready), secrets "Wrapped in perplexed allegories" and raw materials that were essential to the due observance of cultic procedures.

Just as alchemy became discredited and was abandoned as men turned to a systematic, experimental investigation of the world around them, so Christianity has now run its course. At least as elaborate, it has now been exposed as a craft as vain as alchemy. The only difference between the alchemists and the Christians is that the Christians have had a longer run. Both the philosopher's stone and the living stone worshipped by the Christians have proved illusory. In a hundred years' time people will be looking back at Christians as sadly as we look back at the alchemists. "Poor deluded men and women!" they will say. "They gave their allegiance to a fiction. They spent their time in prayer, in singing hymns, in spreading the Gospel. They thought that Christ was King and they sought to widen the bounds of his kingdom. Blind, misguided seekers after eternal truth! We have come to see that whatever man finds supremely worthwhile must come from his own interior resources; they believed in supernatural intervention. We know that there is no eternal rest other than the oblivion that follows death; they thought that mankind had an eternal destiny beyond the grave. We know that truth is not a mystery into which one must grow, but measurement and openness; they thought it was a knowledge of a Supreme Being." If we want to know how Christians will be regarded one hundred years from now, we have only to ask ourselves what we think of the alchemists.

Two groups not far removed from the alchemists also stand to have their reputations reassessed. If the alchemists were

125

victims of their own inordinate ambition — they were trying to solve all problems at one fell swoop — the astrologers were more modest in their aims. Not for them a royal road to wealth, power and life without end; instead they confined their activities to observation of the heavenly bodies, calculation of their conjunctions and the determining of the consequent influence of those bodies upon their clients. To measure the influence of the appropriate heavenly bodies it was necessary to know the date of birth of the subject and if possible the time of birth. It was also necessary to relate the guidance given to the occasion for which advice was required. The astrologer, therefore, was a man giving his time to zodiacal tables, in an attempt to gauge the future course of events. When astrology veered into simple determinism it incurred the disapproval of the Church; while it restricted itself to advising on the choice of propitious moments. for a particular undertaking it was blameless. Thus Chaucer's doctor of physic took care to administer his drugs and potions only when the stars indicated that they had the best chance of success. He would no more neglect this simple precaution than he would neglect to observe the "complexion" or temperament of his patient. The dividing line between medicine and astrology was no more clear than the dividing line between medicine and alchemy.

Magic was another matter. Nowadays magic is a matter of producing rabbits out of top-hats, and conjuring is playing with wands and streamers. At one time, however, it meant much more serious business. The aim of the magician in those days was to influence events by controlling spirits, the sort of thing that Glendower thought himself rather good at in Shakespeare's *Henry the Fourth, Part One*. Some magicians practised black magic, a perverted religious ritual, to secure their ends. Necromancers were amongst these; their special interest was raising the dead. When Faustus in Marlowe's play, *Doctor Faustus*, asks Mephistophilis for a book "wherein I might behold

126

all spells and incantations that I might raise up spirits when I please", what he has in mind is calling up some dead person — Helen of Troy, for example — who will make all the trouble worthwhile.

We make a mistake if we think that these hapless men were further from the goal they so much desired than if they had contented themselves with the consolations of orthodox Christianity. It was the Christians, remember, who had been duped more than anybody else. They actually believed in the religion that had mushroomed out of the mushroom worshippers' imagination. The alchemists, necromancers and astrologists had the advantage of assuming that there were greater secrets in heaven and earth than had been dreamed of in conventional Christian philosophy. They were inspired, perhaps by some lingering tribal memory of ancient mysteries, to search for a stone or elixir that would give wealth and immortality to its discoverer. The fact that they bothered to search, to experiment and to persist shows that they had a better sense of ultimate truth than their fellows who allowed themselves to be fobbed off with an elaborate form of religion far removed from the central mysteries of life, death and rebirth.

Magicians, astrologers and the rest were the natural heirs of the mushroom worshippers. What the alchemists were seeking, although they did not realise it, was the fly agaric. What the astrologer was seeking was the eternal wisdom of which he might gain a glimpse by making use of the fly agaric. What the magician or necromancer was longing for was the power of the mushroom to put him in touch with the wisdom of the underworld, an "angel" to act as a guide and messenger into strange territories. All these misguided enthusiasts, whether honest men or otherwise, were groping for a secret which had once belonged to at least some members of the human race. Had the Romans not stamped out all trace òf the mushroom cult, had there been better philologists in the Middle Ages, had men

127

persevered with the herbs in which they dabbled and taken risks in order to find out exactly what properties the various fungi had, they might have rediscovered an age-old secret. As it was, they floundered around the periphery of the mystery, convinced that there was something to be discovered but knowing nothing of what it might be. While the rest of the world contented itself with the Christian religion, that fudged-up cover for mushroom worship, the alchemists and others persisted in looking for something better. They were right to look but they looked in the wrong place.

If alchemists are reinstated in the era of post-Allegro scholarship, this will be only one of the reversals that will take place. We shall all have to be prepared to do a smart about-turn, to revise not only our religious opinions but many of our historical judgments. Men who have been despised and heaped with ignominy will be found to deserve a place of honour. Men whose judgment has set poets and artists in the foremost rank will be seen to have worked from a false sense of values. Men whose lives showed kindness, generosity and regard for others beyond what is customary will be seen to have been deluded. The mainspring of their lives was inadequate − non-existent, even. They were good men by mistake. Their virtues grew out of a delusion. The implications of Mr Allegro's theory for the common values of civilised life are immense. It is only the fact that we are gradually shaping an open society owing little to traditional assumptions that can spare our blushes in the coming days.

The literature of the Christian era will come to be interpreted in the same fashion as the literature of the ancient Greek era. Men will praise what they find to be good and enduring and abandon all the traditional stuff about Jesus and the Holy Spirit. It will after all signify nothing more than the Greek stories about their gods; we read Greek literature today but we recognise that the Greeks laboured under the misapprehension (or politely appeared to labour under the common misapprehension) that the gods were many in number and only too human in their habits. The majestic structure (or variety of structures) that we call Christian theology will be seen as one of the most intricate structures formed by the human mind; but it will of course be relegated to the same status as the study of old railway time-tables.

If Mr Allegro's theory is correct, we shall be enabled to move at lightning speed to Christian unity – or more correctly to religious unity. Once the claims of Christianity to a unique authoritativeness are dismissed, the way opens up to what R. A. Knox called "reunion all round". There will be no need to discuss the apostolic ministry, or the infallibility of the Pope, or the priesthood of all believers. These issues will have vanished overnight together with traditional Christianity itself. We shall be able to turn to the straightforward task of constructing a grand universal religion, untrammelled by particularities, broad, ample, accommodating. Broad-mindedness will be at a premium; so will statements of an unimpeachable vagueness. We shall no longer be vexed with the problems that have troubled Christendom since the beginning of the Christian era; they will all be solved by the simple expedient of discovering that they never really existed at all.

At the last day the alchemists, magicians and necromancers who have been true to the Great Tradition will rise up and bless the man who vindicated and reinstated them. When all but a fanatic few had written them off, when their theories were matter for polite amusement one man rose up and showed them for what they were. One man proved them to be in the Great Tradition of uncontaminated fertility-worshippers. Though their bones may have crumbled away, their memory can still be honoured. Though their understanding may have been limited and defective, we can still pay tribute to their loyalty and single-mindedness in pursuit of the mushroom.

These are the heroes of religion. At the very least they deserve a place alongside St Patrick, St Francis, St Boniface and King Alfred. When national shrines are reorganised, as they surely must be in the post-Allegro age, the alchemists must be allowed to come into their own. Tardy we may be in recognising their merit; we can make up for our tardiness through the centuries by promptitude and generosity now. In the light of what Mr Allegro tells us we can do nothing else.

As for the rest of us, those who have to carry on the business of the world as it is today, we must plod on with an uncertain goal and a man-made religion. We must hope to be spared bigger and better runways, bigger and noisier jet-planes and bigger and bolder bureaucracies; we must hope that bird-songs and wild flowers will not be entirely eliminated from the land, but beyond that what can we hope for, what can we believe in? Not for us the philosopher's stone, or the elixir of life. That search, we know, leads nowhere but to the mushroom. If the alchemists were unhappy when they had something to search for, how much more unhappy are we who lack even that consolation in the post-Allegro world!

The Same Old Thing

The fact that for nearly two thousand years one religious body has pinned its faith upon not only the existence of the man Jesus, but even upon his spiritual nature and the historicity of certain unnatural events called miracles, is not really relevant to the enquiry.

John M. Allegro, *The Sacred Mushroom and the Cross*

The day after *The Times* published the letter from fifteen scholars dismissing Mr Allegro's book as an essay in fantasy the *Daily Mirror* published in its colour magazine what it entitled: "Our man from Mount Sinai bringing you the new Ten Commandments". The cover of the magazine showed a sombre Moses holding a tablet of the law engraved "Thou shalt do thine own thing". The feature was in fact a racy report on what 825 young people had to say about their attitude to the Ten Commandments. Most of what they had to say was not unexpected, although there did appear to be less reason than most people think for accepting the idea of a generation gap. The conclusion of the matter was as follows: "Thus spake 825 youths and maidens in the year 1970. A distillation of attitudes, moral and spiritual, of one of the liveliest and misjudged young generations of history. We come back to that one composite Commandment with which they might happily replace all Ten: Do your own thing, but, in so doing, do not envy, criticise, or obstruct others from doing theirs. Will anyone care to say what's wrong with that?"

The strongest ally any man can have if he is proposing some novel interpretation of the New Testament is mankind's distaste for the Same Old Thing. A man has no sooner bought a production car than he is calling at the motor accessory shop for nodding dogs, steering-wheel gloves, exhaust-pipe spouts, pseudo-wire wheels and all the other bits and pieces that can make one car look different from another. By such meretricious knick-knacks a car is "personalised"; it attains to custom-built status; though everybody knows that these trimmings do not affect the performance or utility of the car in the slightest ·degree. They merely proclaim the simple-minded owner's readiness to be gulled and cozened into spending money unnecessarily. Shakespeare suffers in the same way. His Romans are dressed like storm-troopers; aspiring producers rearrange the order of his scenes as though they are shuffling a pack of playing cards; there have even been those bold enough to invent happy endings for plays that Shakespeare chose to conclude otherwise. The temptation to improve on Shakespeare is so great as to be irresistible to those who prefer anything – no matter how obvious, trivial or idiosyncratic – to what is familiar and accepted, even if ill understood.

The young woman who varies the length of her skirt or the shape of her body according to the dictates of that mysterious will-o'-the-wisp that we call fashion is another instance of mankind's manner of dealing with the Same Old Thing. From the days of Cleopatra to the days of Jackie Kennedy discerning women have recognised that elegance, far from being an optional extra, is part of being womanly. A carefully assembled wardrobe, a well groomed head of hair, a choice of bangles, beads and cosmetics enable a woman to do what every female ordinarily should do – make herself as attractive as possible (within, one hopes, the bounds of modesty and propriety) to the opposite sex.

Shifts in electoral opinion, changing styles in posters, new methods in education, digital clocks – all can be seen in greater or lesser degree as an avoidance of the Same Old Thing. The merit of the new government, or the new poster, or the new school furniture, or the new time-piece may not be sounder policies, better design, proven efficiency or greater clarity; the merit may be that it makes a change. We find

134

ourselves becoming bored when we are doing the same thing week after week, year after year; we want a change. The change we make may be not in the least beneficial in objective terms, but it answers a need. We are encouraged to make a fresh start and to continue for another stretch. We may have switched from a pattern of proven worth to another pattern of equal or even lesser value; but that is not important. What is important is that we have escaped from the Same Old Thing. The new pattern will serve until it in its turn is replaced. The need for frequent changes of this kind is part of being human.

Mr Allegro, being a scholar, is not driven to his views by a horror of the Same Old Thing, but this is not to say that readers of his latest book will share his academic abstemiousness. Some will hail the mushroom theory with delight just because it is new; others will welcome it because it discomforts exalted (and sometimes pompous) personages; and others will seize an opportunity of bounding at one stride to the heights at present occupied by those dedicated but deluded (as Mr Allegro would have it) men who have been so ill advised as to give their lives to a phantom religion which has now been exposed as a fraud of such monstrous proportions as to deceive the choicest minds of fifty generations and to set the civilisation of Europe and its overseas offspring bowling merrily through the centuries into a cul-de-sac. Mr Allegro is a philologist and it is philology that has compelled him towards certain conclusions that he has daringly set down in black and white; but his strongest ally in commanding a popular audience will undoubtedly be the spectral figure of the Same Old Thing. With the aid of Mr Allegro's philology the man in the traffic jam will be able to exorcise the bogeyman that has so long haunted him in his moral judgments. He will be able to shrug off the claim that man is not on his own and that this life is not everything. He will feel free to enter into a new world delivered from superstition and bondage, liberated from carking anxieties and reverently placed before him to make what he will of it. He will become like a football player free to play on a pitch unspoiled by white lines, free to display his skill without interference from the referee's whistle. The goal into which he is shooting will have no limitations to its dimensions because all these arbitrary and extraneous impositions will have been removed in order to allow him to exercise his anticipation, skill and accuracy as never before. The man in the traffic jam will be given an opportunity of playing a game on an entirely new scale. There will be no troublesome restrictions inherited from the past, no petty infringements to interrupt the wholesome development of his own style of play. All will be his to explore and to create. At last he will have broken into a freedom that he has been longing for since he was first able to choose his own way.

Such is the popular fantasy, mostly concealed, but almost invariably finding expression in strip cartoons in daily newspapers, that will be Mr Allegro's strongest ally in gaining supporters for his theory. The number of people who will be able to pass an informed judgment on the more recondite aspects of his book will be minute. Most will be content to allow those scholars who understand the Semitic and other ancient languages to squabble amongst themselves. But Mr Allegro's book will make a vague and widespread impression to the effect that Christianity as we know it is eyewash, that as far as opinion on matters of Christian dogma goes, Jack is as good as his master, that with the New Testament discredited the man in the traffic jam has opinions on religion every bit as worthwhile as the opinions of any bishop driving fifty miles to conduct a Confirmation service or any minister praying at the bedside of a dying man.

A book such as Mr Allegro's announces the dismissal of the Same Old Thing. Henceforth men are free to invent their own religions and can use the conventional, old-fashioned belief called Christianity purely as a gauge of their efforts, a base line above which any self-respecting do-it-yourself theologian of the seventies ought to be able to rise without any difficulty at all. Men are not only free to invent their own religions; they are free to do without religion altogether. In the past they have not been able to do this without casting anxious glances over their shoulders. There was, after all, always a chance that Christianity might be true and if it was true then some insurance, however slight, against long odds might be in order. But with Christianity altogether discredited, the freedom to pick, choose or totally discard in the religious supermarket is untrammelled. Man has now come of age and has rid himself of what has dogged his steps through the centuries, the uneasy possibility that Christianity is true, that heaven and hell are alternatives open to all men. Man is now liberated from subservience and deference to the Same Old Thing. A new age has dawned. Hallelujah — or something like that.

There is a good deal to flatter man's vanity in the idea that a religion that has satisfied former generations is not good enough for his own. It is gratifying to think that one's own standards are so much higher than those of one's predecessors, and it appears enriching and rewarding to contemplate new possibilities of progress unknown to past generations. A vague acceptance of the idea of mankind making progress on all fronts has characterised a good many of the favoured periods in human history. Provided one ignores the fact that the great achievements of the human mind have come apparently arbitrarily from many periods, there is a good deal that carries conviction in the idea of all-round progress — particularly if you happen to have grown up in a home without an inside lavatory and now cannot bear to live without central heating. It is easy to feel sympathy with such a person as Lord Trenchard who was not content that anything should be unaltered simply because things had always been done in a particular way. When he was rebuked for expressing unorthodox ideas on religious symbolism, he told the Archbishop of Canterbury, Dr Fisher, that the Archbishop's trouble was that he imagined all religion stopped when Christ was crucified.

Nevertheless, a theologian who proposes an entirely novel reinterpretation of the Christian faith must expect to be regarded with a generous measure of scepticism. The fact that the Churches have grown old and dull, the fact that Christianity is no longer a novelty, the fact that we all welcome something out of the ordinary to make a break in our routine, these things should not be allowed to moderate the healthy scepticism that should be reserved for Mr Allegro's theory about the origins of Christianity. There is no quick, easy, painless way of avoiding the Same Old Thing. It is precisely because Christianity continues to be the Same Old Thing that it is the faith for all generations.

Christians are expected to believe that Christianity makes unique claims, but they are not of course required to believe that Christianity is unique in the sense of being entirely different from any other religion known to mankind. Nor are Christians required to believe that all other religions are 100 per cent wrong. Orthodox Christians believe that God spoke to mankind in his Son, and that when men begin to understand who Jesus was, a great many things begin to click into place. God's Son came into a world in which men half-understood, and even three-quarters understood a great deal about God's nature. Hints and flashes of understanding abounded in the ancient world, not least in the mystery religions. Those who preached the Gospel did not deny or discredit this partial understanding. They explained that in Christ God had fully revealed himself, so that men who had seen Jesus could say they had seen the Father. In the light of this, former opinions and

138

beliefs were modified. Instead of shadows there was the light of the noonday sun. Instead of hesitant speculation there was cast-iron conviction. For many people there still is, despite Mr Allegro's assertions. Many are still persuaded of the truth of the apostolic Gospel, or, to put it another way, of the Same Old Thing.

The Same Old Thing is not easily dismissed. A faith that has survived for nineteen centuries has not done so by holding to an inadequate or superficial view of the human predicament. Orthodox Christianity has always looked unblinkingly at man's startling capacity to be both an ape and an angel, and the unflattering estimation of man together with the immoderate care given to him by his Creator and Redeemer has won the allegiance of men and women from the bullying days of Nero and his minions to the contemptuous days of post-Christian "enlightenment". The survival power of the Same Old Thing beggars description. Everybody knows exactly what Christianity stands for; it is impossible for it to spring any surprises after all these years, but it continues to claim the songs and spirits of generation after generation of young people because it goes nearer the heart of things than any other view of life at present available. The more one looks at it, the more one concludes that the Same Old Thing is a finely balanced piece of metaphysical machinery with every part, large or tiny, exactly shaped and exactly placed. It has the momentum and the immobility of a giant gyroscope. In the midst of man's confusion it points unerringly, as does a gyroscopic compass, to that star whose worth's unknown, though his height be taken. The man who would despise the Christian faith as we have traditionally known it because it is merely the Same Old Thing is the kind of man who would laugh at the Pole Star for always being in the same place in the heavens. More reflective men know better.

Spring is the same old thing each year, but we welcome it

none the less. We do not wish that daffodils were anything but yellow; neither do we hanker after red snowdrops or blue celandines. When the horse chestnut buds become sticky we do not wish them otherwise; we welcome the stickiness just as we welcome the forsythia and the wallflowers because they foreshadow happier, warmer days after the endurance test of winter. To accept the round of the seasons and to welcome a new beginning to the year is as old as man; this kind of acceptance is part of being human. Without such acceptance there is no genuine maturity.

The Bible is the Same Old Thing as it was a thousand years ago. The church calendar — whatever version we may favour — has been very much the same for hundreds of years. There may be room for more honesty in church music and church architecture, but once the primitive confession "Jesus is Lord" had been formulated, orthodoxy was set to develop in such a way as to deny the possibility of novelty. But if it lacked novelty, it had stability, and the endurance of orthodox belief as the Same Old Thing over a succession of centuries has invested Christian belief with something of the permanence of the annual return of spring.

Orthodox Christianity makes no bones about being the Same Old Thing. It glories in its unchanging nature. "Jesus Christ is the same yesterday, today and for ever," says the writer to the Hebrews. Of course it is true that just as a woman must take pains to vary her costume and appearance if she is not to gain a reputation for unimaginative dowdiness, so the orthodox Christian must ensure that the lordship of the unchanging Christ is expressed in meaningful terms in each generation. This we often fail to do, and religion becomes distasteful as a result. But just as a woman does not set out to make a series of caricatures of the female form, so a Christian believer does not seek to mangle the New Testament Gospel. Like a woman who dresses tastefully, he seeks to enhance what is given.

Orthodox Christian belief is the Same Old Thing because it meets the needs of the same old mankind. Whatever technological or other achievements may have characterised any particular age in the history of mankind, men have been remarkably similar. They have been torn between greed and generosity, loyalty and treachery, kindness and cruelty from generation to generation. If this were not so, we should find the psalms untrue to our own experience; we should find Joseph an incomprehensible character; we should dismiss Noah and his ark from our minds and from our children's toy-boxes. But we do not find these passages from the Old Testament meaningless or irrelevant. Each time we read them we find our own nature more clearly reflected in them. We find that the psalmist and Joseph and Noah have more affinities with us than we care to admit. Though our world may be very different from theirs, in essential characteristics we are one.

The Christian holds to an orthodox pattern of belief because in the first place this is the only reasonable way to think about God at all (who after all wants a God he cannot respect?) and because Jesus Christ showed men that God is actually like this. We consider the Son of God as he appears in the Gospels and there is an uncanny actuality about it all. This is what God would be like, this is how God would behave, if he with all the qualities we have mentioned actually did come down amongst us. God would not be a ranter; nor would he be a mere idealist. He would not pay attention merely to ostensibly important people and he would not flinch at saying hard things. He would have time for people. He would surprise people by the things he said and did. He would be positive, creative, encouraging. He would be inexplicable. This is exactly the kind of impression that the Jesus of the Gospels makes upon us. He is warm, human – and different. We have a feeling that he has made this impression on every generation since he came. We know that it is not novelty that commands the allegiance of people in

141

every generation; it is truth and all that is ultimate appearing in the midst of the human race.

When nothing will sell unless it is "new"; when a new pack is almost as effective a selling point as a new product; when the appearance of originality confers prestige; in days such as these the appeal of the Same Old Thing is strictly limited. Stability, continuity and solidity are of less account than superficial novelty. Men and women who can be persuaded to put tigers into their tanks without bothering to look into octanes and additives and the technology of the fractionating column will easily be persuaded to switch from one brand of religion to another if the new brand is excitingly packaged. Mr Allegro has produced an excitingly packaged reinterpretation of the New Testament; for many people a thorough examination of the merits of that reinterpretation will be of little importance. What will be important will be the opportunity of a change of brand loyalty, from a religion that is tough, precise and demanding to a religion without rules, a religion without doctrines, a religion without God.

A mushroom a day

The repeated bouts of drug-stimulated excitement were in the nature of violent and unnaturally prolonged sexual orgasms, whether or not they resulted in erection and ejaculation on the part of the men or spasmodic vaginal contractions by the woman.

John M. Allegro, *The Sacred Mushroom and the Cross*

If man's distaste for the Same Old Thing is the first thing that is likely to make him welcome an approach to Christianity that turns it inside-out, the second most telling factor in gaining his approval for a new theory is man's readiness for anything that promises sexual freedom. The man who decorates his car to disguise the fact that it is virtually the same as the cars one million other men are driving is a man who will be delighted to entertain fantasies in which he possesses an oriental harem, the numerous occupants of which will provide the same pleasure for him with only the slightest variations. The man in the traffic jam knows that sexual activity provides dependable pleasure and he is happy to find some formula which will allow him to maximise his pleasure without unpleasant after- or side-effects. Whereas he likes to pretend that his car is different from every other car on the road, he likes his sexual partner or partners to be dependably voluptuous, wholesomely lusty. He is seeking what Ben Jonson's alchemist was looking for, a chance to renew

Our youth and strength, with drinking the elixir,
And so enjoy a perpetuity
Of life and lust.

A theologian who proposes a new doctrine that will give the man in the traffic jam the opportunity of heightening his sexual pleasure with the approval of religion will be sure of a welcome. The man who suggests that Christianity is really a heavily dis-

145

guised fertility religion which ought to have its camouflage stripped off so that men can enjoy the freedom which narrow-minded religious leaders have denied to them is likely to be hailed as a second Martin Luther. This is precisely the kind of news that people are agog to hear; to mix religion with sexual licence is good news indeed for modern man. This kind of news has always been good news for man — which is precisely why the worship of Venus or Diana succeeded for so long in Paphos or Ephesus. Worship by means of sexual indulgence is the kind of worship which the man in the traffic jam can wholeheartedly enter into. To enjoy strippers and prostitutes without the disapproval of society at large is good; to enjoy strippers and prostitutes and know that one is being truly religious at the same time is even better.

A resurgence of interest in fertility rites is no unlikely event in the 1970s. If we flatter ourselves that we have developed beyond these primitive, atavistic impulses, we need look no further than the nearest bookstall. There we shall find daily papers, women's magazines and more specialised publications giving space to horoscopes (cast with or without the aid of a computer); we shall find savagery and superstition minutely described for four and six a time; we shall find the techniques of sex, sex straight and crooked, minutely discussed for the benefit of a generation that finds no bliss more convincing than the moment of physical ecstasy and no bliss more worth paying for. With such a scale of values the possibility of a new-style fertility religion coming to birth is far from inconceivable. A religion that replaces Calvary passion by sexual passion, baptism death and rebirth by sexual expiry and recovery, the Holy Spirit by human semen, plainsong by throbbing sex-songs and life beyond the grave by a plunge into the eternal female is a religion that the man of the 1970s is likely to find custom-built for him. When a provincial evening paper that is something of a trend-setter can splash a review of *A Programmed Guide to*

146

Seduction (how to get your girl-friend out of her bra, etc.) with a photograph of a girl displaying breasts covered with nothing more substantial than a strip of computer-tape, a mindless fertility religion with dolly-girls acting as temple prostitutes and worshippers meeting to munch, imbibe or inhale an aphrodisiac of incredible potency is not so remote a possibility as might at first be thought.

To a large extent, of course, we orthodox Christians have only ourselves to blame for making a fertility religion seem desirable. We have so consistently failed to give sex its proper place that it appears to be the property of those who reject religious dogma. The Church has come to be regarded as disapproving of the idea of deriving pleasure from sexual intercourse. The result is that the Church has seemed not only to set its face against cultic prostitution and licensed promiscuity but to suggest that sexual relations of any kind are best hushed up. If they cannot actually be abolished, the best thing to do is to pretend that they never take place.

Those who are credulous enough to accept this view find certain parts of the Old Testament extremely embarrassing. The Song of Solomon, for example, is a tender, explicit, lusty and gorgeously colourful avowal of sexual love (when interpreted in a pre-Allegro sense). The words have lost nothing of their ardour in the course of two or three thousand years. The tone is a thousand miles removed from the withered utterances of elderly religious leaders; what we meet as we read the poem is the burning desire shared by a lover and his lass, a desire that is physical, unhampered by elderly tut-tuttings and impatient for love's climacteric. The desire of the one for the other is all-engrossing, yet utterly tender. The force of appetite is matched by depth of consideration. These two have no need of aphrodisiacs to heighten their desire; it is marvellous, mighty and irresistible.

If it is foolish for us religious people to deny sex and to

suggest that religious faith and sexual activity are incompatible, it is equally foolish to fail to attend to the sexual content of the Bible. The patriarchs, for example, appear to have been men of exceptional sexual powers. The Bible is in fact very far from being a book without any sexual aspect. The men and women we meet in its pages are very much like us as we know ourselves to be in our more honest moments.

It would not be fair to Mr Allegro to say that he has, Ali Baba-like, opened up the door to a cave of bliss and invited his fellow human beings to enter. Mr Allegro is not proposing that anybody should take up the pristine mystery religion that was so grievously distorted by the early Christians. He is not urging men to gain sexual enjoyment and religious awareness by taking fly agaric instead of alcohol. Whatever else he is doing, Mr Allegro is not casting himself for the role of a new prophet, or the founder of a new religion. Mr Allegro is a philologist and he is drawing conclusions in the light of the philological material he has collected. But academic philologist as he is, Mr Allegro is putting forward a theory which is likely to have practical repercussions, and these cannot be ignored.

By discrediting the traditional interpretation of the New Testament and showing Christianity as it has always been understood to be nothing more than a perverted form of fertility religion, Mr Allegro has invited his readers to give attention to the underlying sexual patterns connected with the mushroom. Nobody is likely to attempt to re-establish the mushroom cult in the way that enthusiasts conduct steam traction rallies or stage-coach journeys. It is unlikely that the Churches will replace their regular services of worship by meetings at which the mushroom will be exposed and eaten. A more likely consequence of Mr Allegro's book is a willingness to let the older people get on with their traditional Christianity while the more go-ahead section of the population take their place as successors of the original mushroom worshippers. As they take their place in this succession the go-ahead ones can disarm criticism from their more orthodox friends by pointing out that they, the go-ahead ones, are nearer the truth of the New Testament than anybody else.

What Mr Allegro has done is not merely to give a full and open acknowledgment of the place of sex in the life of the religious person; he has made possible a take-over bid for the entire Christian religion on behalf of sex. Or, to be more accurate, he has argued that the entire fabric of Christianity is a mere ruse to provide a vehicle for the transmission of secrets which, when known, introduce the initiated ones to vast areas of sexual experience whose existence has been unknown to the vast majority during most of the world's history. Beneath the panoply of Christian history, behind the austere deductions of scholars, underneath the compelling narrative of the Gospels is a recipe for more intense sexual delight, for new heights of ecstasy, for bigger and better orgasms. The story of Jesus and the tribulations of Paul were a mere cover which enabled men who took their pleasures seriously to pass on their aphrodisiac treasure-hoard. Instead of being enriching and ennobling documents sufficient to captivate and redirect the most flagrant sinner, the Gospels become no more than an interesting side-effect produced by men anxious to get on with their sexual activity themselves and anxious to ensure that subsequent generations were not enticed away from the sexual activity which they themselves believed to be the primary occupation for any normal man.

If Mr Allegro is right, it may be argued that all the talk about faith, hope and charity is so much hot air. What really matters is not man's relationship with his Creator and his fellow-men, but his sexual activity. The story of the Good Samaritan is as nothing compared with heightened sexual awareness. The Prodigal Son was foolish not because he stayed in the far country feeding swine when he might have been back at home with his father; he was foolish because he failed to develop his capacity for sexual enjoyment to match his sexual powers. Instead of feeding swine and ruminating upon his own short-sightedness, he should have been munching sacred mushrooms and making gargantuan demands of all the girls in that part of the world. The lame tales which we call parables sink to the level of the jokes that decorate the margins of boys' comic papers when we compare them with the adult message which they were intended to conceal. While we puzzle over the implications of the story of the foolish virgins we ought to be discovering what a foolish and unrewarding way of life virginity is. While we ponder the story of the importunate widow, we ought to be admonishing widows of our acquaintance to get their teeth into the mushroom that will restore their jaded appetite and send them eagerly not to their onerous responsibilities but to the nearest male who can satisfy their demands. Mankind has been deluded by all this theological small-talk. It was never meant to be taken seriously. We are merely the last in a long succession of generations that have tamely accepted the Gospels as the oracles of God when we should, if we had had our wits about us, been out looking for mushrooms. How can we have been so blind? The mushroom has been beckoning us through the ages; its devotees in preceding generations have given us careful if cryptic directions to ensure that we do not miss this greatest of all secrets. Yet all the time, when we might have been stimulating our sexual appetite to undreamed of heights, when we might have been enjoying ecstasies beyond those normally experienced by mankind, we have been blindly, foolishly, perversely imagining that a better thing to do was to believe on the Lord Jesus Christ and receive the power of the Holy Spirit. To what depths can man fall when he ignores the ever-present fulfilment of his desires in a lovers' clinch and sets compassion above conquest! What muddled perverseness he shows in preferring prayer and fasting to the exhaustion of sated lust! What folly to value faith, hope and charity above private passion and sexual fulfilment! How grateful we should be that the secret of the sacred mushroom is secret no longer! Truly a great honour has been reserved to Mr Allegro in that he above all the academics on earth should have unlocked the mystery and once again made it possible for men to turn from the vain pursuit of metaphysical truth and peace of conscience to the more rewarding pursuit of unrestrained sexual enjoyment.

What we must do now, it may be said, is to go along to the local greengrocer or herbalist and lay in a store of sacred mushrooms. Dark cellars which have hitherto been used merely for the production of culinary mushrooms destined to find their way into a mixed grill or a steak, kidney and mushroom pie will now be turned over to the production of this bigger, better mushroom. Market gardeners who have been content to supply mushrooms to the greengrocer and to the canning factory will now work from new spores. No more rows of dull grey fungi resembling malformed turnips or potatoes; instead, acre upon acre of the colourful spotted mushrooms destined to rejuvenate tired husbands, lovers and mistresses.

Prayer? Sacrament? Bible study? So much waste of time. Up, up, my friend, come leave your books. Fall to eating the sacred mushroom. Mushrooms give a man a sense of proportion. Nothing is more healthy than mushrooms. A mushroom-eating party will give a man − or a woman − new perspectives. Don't bother with attempting to know God; he doesn't exist. He was dreamed up by desperate mushroom-munchers who saw their supplies running out and were anxious to put by their recipe for better times. If you must have some kind of religion, first munch your mushroom. You will be in the true succession of those single-minded men who, in times of tribulation, when refugees were streaming past, when the enemy were at their heels, knew that their prime responsibility was to preserve the secret of the mushroom so that succeeding generations should not be side-tracked into spiritual religion or self-forgetful ethics but should first munch their mushroom and then go out to get a woman with child. Here is the secret of the ages, open for all to read: munch the mushroom and intensify your sexual ecstasy. What man can reasonably expect more in the way of everlasting wisdom? Mr Allegro has certainly not invited men to indulge, and would not approve of their doing so, but the mushroom now beckons.

Glory be to fecundity?

The etymological explanation of the chief god-names that is now possible supports this view, pointing to a common theme of life-giving, fecundity. Thus the principal gods of the Greeks and Hebrews, Zeus and Yahweh (Jehovah), have names derived from the Sumerian meaning "juice of fecundity", spermatozoa, "seed of life".

John M. Allegro, *The Sacred Mushroom and the Cross*

Mr Allegro does not of course believe that God spoke to man. He says as much in the opening sentences of his introduction. Religion was born not out of a self-disclosure of God but out of the self-dissatisfaction of man. Man's problem was not to know the unknowable or to listen for the divine voice; man's problem was to establish communication with the source of the world's fertility. At first man set out to control that source; later he came to recognise that co-operation was a wiser pattern than control. But all along God was remote, passive, impersonal. The possibility that God might be leading a self-sufficient existence, that he might be a person with a will and a purpose, that he might have his own views on the creatures who were so deeply concerned with the propagation of animal and plant life does not seem to have entered Mr Allegro's head; it has certainly not entered his book. The story of the sacred mushroom is the story of a search for ultimate fertility. What is being sought is not an encounter with a living being in whose likeness we ourselves are made but a tapping of primeval energy, an energy more vast and potent than that found in the fossil fuels, more stupendous than any giant's sexual drive, more terrifying than that seen in the sun.

The god of the mushroom theory is not of any great consequence to his followers except as a source of power. He does not make inconvenient moral demands of his followers; nor does he call them to sacrifice and care for others. He is the fount of fecundity, the original male. His virtue is his sexual capacity. The mushroom worshippers' God was a god of both parts and passions, for sexual activity was his forte, and it is his sublime and unquenchable sexuality that makes him the goal to which his believers aspire. As they partake through the mushroom rites of his unbounded, prodigal, zestful, amoral potency they catch a vision of him. Not for them any labouring under the misapprehension that it is the pure in heart that shall see God; the truth of the matter is that it is the sexually potent, the men and women who have drunk the nectar of the gods, the juice of the mushroom, who will see him. Religious insight comes not from prayer and fasting, not from meditation on the determined, inexplicable self-giving which we see in the life of Jesus, but from a taste of mushrooms. The fulfilment of the heavenly vision is sexual before it is spiritual. The man who would see God must enjoy the liberating potency that comes from aphrodisiac dieting. Only then will his eyes be opened. But when his eyes are opened, what will he see? A being recognisably personal, a being with a will and purpose of his own, a self-existent beneficent Creator, a being who delights in mending and repairing creatures so misguided as to spoil themselves, created though they are in the likeness of their Creator? Not a bit of it. He will see a god of immense reproductive power, blind, hungry and frenzied, careless of the individual units that we call men and women, concerned only with the unending task of impregnation, gestation and parturition, solving all problems by bringing to birth multitude upon multitude of living things. This is a god whose final purpose for mankind is a way of defeating some of man's age-old enemies — famine, war, drought — and the way of victory is multiplication. Multiply, multiply, says this god. Worship by population explosion. There is no alternative to obliteration but multiplication, for what can please a fertility god more than conception after conception, birth after birth, teeming wombs and overflowing maternity wards?

Man does not know what God is like; he can only guess. And man's best guessing is peculiarly unrewarding. Even in these enlightened days, Mr Allegro tells us, we worship a God who is named after a man's penis. Our conceptions of his nature may be more developed than the crude ideas of our Sumerian ancestors, but we who believe the Christian faith are· the final inheritors of a tradition practising the worship of a divine penis that sprays the earth with its semen and hides itself in a mushroom. Aldous Huxley with his mescalin was nearer to the original form of "Christianity" than any of us conventional believers. Those who want to find this God must eat a poison that we warn our children against.

The character of the god who emerges from the pages of *The Sacred Mushroom and the Cross* is amoral. He is a god of fecundity. In so far as he has any purpose intelligently conceived it is the sheer multiplication of living things. Quality is of no consequence. That human beings should develop such virtues as loyalty, patience, kindness, compassion is of no consequence to the god of fecundity. These are no more than sidelines, trimmings to the matter of being a prolific human. The god found in Mr Allegro's book is a god invented by man himself, a god invented by weary and sated men who dreamed, not like Rupert Brooke's fish of "wetter water, slimier slime" but of unending sexual ecstasy, of a heaven where passion never fades and where the god looks down benevolently on myriad upon myriad of his creatures endlessly, tirelessly copulating.

Is this a god worth having? Is it worth giving time and thought to religion if the best we can achieve is a deity representing our own sexual vigour? Need we bother with a god who can so easily be imagined and who is already being represented on all sides in the world today? It is a truism that novelists, playwrights and epic poets can more easily create characters of less moral worth than themselves than they can create characters of ripe goodness. Can we not say that the same is true of

157

religion, that any god invented by man himself will be a defective god, a god not deserving worship? Is it not true to say that only a god who reveals himself, who surprises us, who speaks and commands us can deserve our worship? Mushroom worship does not lead to the God who reveals himself. It leads to the exaltation of animal appetite, the enthronement of lubricity, the deification of desire. If this is the only god there is we can get on very well without him; we have perfectly adequate fertility rites of our own, thank you very much; herbal remedies went out with Grandma, thank you very much again; when we select our aphrodisiacs, we like them to have proper scientific names like LSD or mescalin, not a crude cabbage-like name like mushroom.

The mushroom worshipper's god is a congenial being. More sexual awareness, he cries! Multiply the phallic symbols! Fill the aching wombs! Enjoy ecstasy oftener! Here is a god with a message men are glad to receive. No unpleasant instructions about avoiding lying and cheating, no rebukes to human pride and self-sufficiency, no divine request to have first place. This god tells men to get on with what they most desire to do. He himself will help them in their efforts, for this is the field within which his own ability is pre-eminent; indeed no other field interests him. At last man has the god he has always desired, a comforting, unjudging companion who understands all about desires that cannot be denied and flowers that must be plucked before they fade. No god could be more acceptable. And yet. . . and yet. . . man is well able to manage by himself. He does not need a god like this. Mushroom juice, yes – anything that makes the act more pleasurable, but why bother to bring religion into it? We all know it is in the genes and in the mind.

If this is the only god we can have in the twentieth century then better by far to be without any god at all. Better by far to be an honest humanist, painfully exploring the human predicament without expecting any outside help, painfully building what appears to be true and beautiful and worthwhile here in this life because we know that only our works will survive while we perish and are forgotten. If God is not an independent being capable of revealing himself and speaking to his creatures; if the Manufacturer has given no instructions to his creatures and is nowhere to be found; if the only possible god is a god without even the resolution of Milton's Satan, indeed without any character at all; if the only possible god is dumb, inert and less than human, if all these things are true, then we are better off without him. He has nothing to give us, and we waste our time thinking that he wants anything we have to give except sexual performance.

Of course Mr Allegro is not suggesting — and it would be ungenerous to credit him with suggesting — that we should resuscitate a forgotten fertility cult and begin to make amends for our long period of indifference to the divine fertility principle which is the best we can expect to know in the way of a deity. The reader of *The Sacred Mushroom and the Cross* ends up believing, if he allows himself to be convinced by the argument of the book, that religion of any kind is old hat. We should be above needing any kind of god at all. God does not matter; we must give our attention to moral principles, and particularly to those moral principles which are of self-evident worth, whether they come from the book of Exodus or the Code of Hammurabai. We cannot say "Glory be to fecundity"; fecundity has now been analysed and computerised and we can promote or curb fecundity in a way that would have astonished the mushroom worshippers. The mystery has been taken out of fertility; pills, hormones, research stations and clinics have made possible what ancient man most desired, the ability to select an appropriate fertility level for man and beast alike and to order the weight of crops, the extent of wild life and the human population as may be most convenient. There is nothing here

159

to deserve man's worship; man has got past that kind of thing.

Mr Allegro invites us to consider what kind of God we believe in. Can we say that the God we know is better than the outmoded fecundity god? The character of God is, after all, the determining factor in religion. Believe in a god who welcomes child sacrifice and you will become a child sacrificer. Believe in an erratic, unpredictable tyrant and you will become a creature of impulse and fearfulness. The same principle holds all the way through. The man who believes God to be the majestic lawgiver, the predestinator, the unchallengeable, remote controller of the universe, is dangerously likely to develop a harsh, severe and inhuman outlook. Such a person is likely to be uncommonly persevering, but he is also likely to be implacable and unrelenting. The man who gives undue weight to the conception of God as a beneficent creator is likely to believe that beauty is truth, truth beauty. He is likely to be to some extent insensible of moral issues and to regard religion as a mild, luminous aura attaching automatically to all human endeavours. Nothing is more important than the character of the god that a man believes in. "What kind of a god do you believe in?" is as important as "Do you believe in God?"

It is not very exciting to reaffirm traditional belief. We have heard it said so many times that the God of the Christian revelation is the God of patience and loving-kindness described so tenderly in Isaiah 40, for example, the God of love and forgiveness whom we find represented in the story of the Prodigal Son (or the story of the two sons, as we are better advised to call it), the God of judgment before whom we shall all stand to give an account of ourselves. Here is a God of purpose and compassion and the depth of the compassion is seen in the cross of Christ. It is the cross that makes Christianity something more than a version of an existing fertility cult. It is the cross that makes Christianity something more than a synthesis of all that is best in Mithraism, the cult of Demeter and the mystery of Orphis.

A faith that is a man-made amalgam or an improvement on the trendiest of religious options is not a faith worth committing one's life to.

The case for Christianity is that it is something revealed, something that could not have been guessed or contrived, something given. Christianity is not a development engineered by man; it is the result of God confronting and speaking to his creatures. Christianity is not a matter of man doing his best to get in touch with whatever god there may be; it is a matter of God showing his favour to man and reaching down to lift him up to God's level. Christianity is not a painfully slow climb by man into God's presence; it is God shining through the clouds and darkness to give man a glimpse of himself. Christianity is a personal God taking the initiative to introduce men to himself.

There is a difference between the reflective or creative man trying to give expression to something he has seen or half-seen in a new way, trying to find the right words, or the right colours, or the right notes to grasp, pin down and fix his moment of vision so that others can see it too, there is a difference between such a man and the man whose only stock-in-trade is novelty, who puts a meretricious gloss on plaster-board or manufactures slogans or exploits human weakness by garish displays. The person whose taste runs to novelty at any price will find the God to whom Christians pay homage a very disappointing God indeed. "The same yesterday and today and for ever" is a character all at odds with the brisk, newer-than-new tastes of the 1970s. Who wants a God who hasn't changed since Waterloo? Who wants a God who exactly matched the Victorian era? But it is not that God has not changed since Waterloo. He has not changed since Stonehenge was laboriously erected. He has not changed since the earth spun out into orbit. He has not changed since he worked with his slide-rule and dividers to express his creative instinct back at square one.

The God worshipped by Christians is Almighty but there are

limits to what he can do. By his nature God cannot be the author of nonsense. He cannot make two and two add up to five. He cannot order a thing to be in more than one place at a time. He cannot turn himself into a toadstool, and he cannot renounce his past history and start all over again from square one. God is above this kind of tomfoolery. It is this as much as anything else which makes him God. Those who want a god who can act the magician, sport like the Greek godlings, and show himself as up-to-the-minute as any publicist can make their own god. They will doubtless find their own invention more congenial than the God to whom Christians bow the knee.

If God is there at all, he is the kind of God to whom Christians have traditionally bowed the knee. With the men in every generation who have paused to think about the matter, we kneel in homage. We are not so busy changing God to fit our own conceptions of what he ought to be that we neglect to consider him as he has shown himself to us.

The latest news about soap powder or trading stamps is not impressive to the man looking down from the top of Everest — or for that matter from the top of Popacapetl. The latest theory about the beginnings of religious experience is not very impressive when one is looking into the eyes of a child full of wonder. The latest idea about God is not very helpful to a man who has lost his children in a fire. The Christian believes that God not only exists but has an imagination of such scope that da Vinci is no more than a pavement artist by comparison. The Christian believes that God not only exists but has a capacity for instantaneous processing and attention that makes the most rapid and multi-channelled computer look as slow as Lewis Carroll's dormouse. The Christian believes that God not only exists but has compassion which makes all the good Samaritans who have ever lived look as unmoved as monoliths from Easter Island.

Has God spoken or is the best that man can do to pursue a

162

search for a silent, withdrawn God? Is God like the Inland Revenue office to which we send carefully composed letters only to receive in reply a scribbled note on a slip of pulp paper? Are we mistaken to suppose that the God to whom we pray is a God who is less human than we are, less able to speak his mind, a mere shadow of a God? Mr Allegro seems to proceed from the assumption that this is the only kind of God it is possible to believe in after one has eliminated the fanciful expectations of the myth-makers. The cavortings round the mushroom and the deluded sharing of bread and wine are alike mistaken because both sets of worshippers believe that God is active, vocal and accessible. It is at this early point that the orthodox Christian must take issue with Mr Allegro. God does not merely exist. He has spoken and acted. He is Creator, Redeemer, Encourager. He is more personal than the most commanding human personality. He has revealed himself in Christ. The human creatures for whom he has such amazing affection will one day stand before him to give an account of themselves. Glory be to fecundity? No, glory be to the Trinity!

Mushroom Messiah?

In the phallic mushroom, the "man-child" born of the "virgin" womb, we have the reality behind the Christ figure of the New Testament story.

John M. Allegro, *The Sacred Mushroom and the Cross*

If a man accepts the mushroom cult interpretation of the New Testament, then he must also accept as a corollary the notion of Jesus as a mushroom Messiah, a nine days wonder, a flash in the pan. On this view Jesus is not a commanding figure exacting awe and obedience from one generation after another; he is a tailor's dummy dressed up and tricked out by a hard-pressed generation of mushroom cult followers to divert the attention of inquisitive policemen from the secrets of the mushroom. Jesus, if he ever existed, had his biography cooked and his script rewritten to make it appear that he, and not the sacred mushroom, was the centre of attention. His name was chosen because it happened to provide opportunities for word-play. His friends were invented and given names for similar reasons. The crucifixion and resurrection were no more than broad hints about an underground mystery religion. If there happens to be merit in the ethical teaching of the New Testament it is there not because the teaching comes from the Son of God (he probably never existed) but because it commends itself to the reader.

Every man must decide for himself whether this is a conceivable view of Jesus. Those who have encountered Christ and have knelt before the ascended King and Saviour can have no doubt about their reply. What a man finds today when he seriously seeks out God is the person whom people met in Capernaum nineteen centuries ago when they seriously sought to know God. The man who has encountered Christ is convinced that he has met a person of honesty, clarity and author-ity. What he knows of Christ is consistent with what he knows of men at large and what he knows of life and its issues.

We all tend to see such a matter in personal terms. I mention honesty because it seems to me that this is one of the pre-occupations of the good newspaperman. He wants to find out the truth. But truth is elusive and it is sometimes deliberately overlaid. The newspaperman may have to find his way through the institutional defence mechanisms — guarded statements, "helpful" hand-outs, the befriending tactics of public relations officers and others who court, flatter and attempt to bamboozle in an effort to preserve the good name of the institution they represent. He may be rebuffed as I remember one diocesan bishop irritably rebuffing a press inquiry with the words "I'm having my lunch!" as he slammed the receiver down. The news-paperman will have to ask half a dozen people for their versions of the story or their view of the matter and be prepared to upset four of them if the evidence seems to point that way. The newspaperman who has had to cut his way through tangles to the heart of the matter, to a position where he can express the truth as he sees it, will inevitably lose erstwhile friends as year succeeds to year. Words published without trimmings by an independent person are rarely received with a warm welcome. The newspaperman's honesty costs him something.

The Church is an institution and it no more welcomes honest assessment than any other institution. For a man in a respon-sible position to talk straightforwardly about the position of Christianity in western society and about his own private beliefs is costly to the individual and embarrassing to the institution.

The man who has grown accustomed to seeking out the truth in current matters (rather than the façade which interested parties have erected to make their version of the truth seem more attractive) finds himself coming to entertain a profession-al's admiration for Jesus. He gained a reputation amongst insti-

tutional leaders for being awkward. He was an extremely uncomfortable companion for the Pharisees for instance. When he
put them on the spot in respect of their attitude to the Sabbath,
for example, he brought the true significance of their teaching
into the open and made them squirm with discomfort. If, he
said, they allowed animals to be cared for on the Sabbath, was
it not reasonable that men should be looked after too? They
had no reply to make. Jesus had exposed the hollowness of
their case; he had also helped them to see the truth about themselves. Simon the Pharisee was another who saw himself in a
new light after a conversation with Jesus. Before meeting Jesus
he had hardly recognised that he stood in need of forgiveness
at all; the careful performance of his religious duties had blinded
him to the idea that he and the prostitute who washed Jesus'
feet were both on a level as far as coming short of God's glory
was concerned. It was not until Jesus told him a story about
two men who had their debts cancelled that he saw himself in
a true unflattering light for the first time.

Again, when the rich young ruler approached Jesus and pro-
tested his deep desire to enjoy eternal life, Jesus helped him to
an honest recognition of his position by inviting him to give up
what he valued most in life, his property and money. The young
man went away disappointed, but he had learned something
about himself.

When Mrs Zebedee came forward and requested the foremost
places in the government of Christ's kingdom for her two boys
(to put it in present-day terms she was asking that one should
be made Chancellor of the Exchequer and the other Foreign
Secretary), Jesus first pointed out that such favours were not
his to bestow, and he also pointed out that Mrs Zebedee was
mistaken about the nature of true greatness. To understand
what that is, he said on other occasions, men have to consider
the greatest man ever born to a woman, John the Baptist, and —
unexpected and disconcerting suggestion — a child.

In his determination to get things clear, to see things for what they were and to enable others to see things straight in their turn, Jesus was demonstrating the virtues that the newspaperman finds particularly attractive. He was being honest. He was also of course insisting that the honesty that was appropriate in inquiring into matters of general interest should also be in evidence in a man's private opinions. In this respect Jesus was foreshadowing Shakespeare's Polonius: "This above all, To thine own self be true, And it must follow as the night the day, Thou canst not then be false to any man." The first step in religion, he was saying, was to be true to oneself. Whatever one concludes about the person of Jesus as the God-man, one cannot fail to admire the honesty of him. The world is a better place for this kind of honesty wherever it appears.

Another point about Jesus that strikes somebody who has worked amongst newspapermen is his clarity. He made himself understood. He made words work. He was a skilled practitioner in the newspaperman's own field. In common everyday words he expressed profound understanding of human issues. A plank in the eye, a camel through the eye of a needle (or perhaps as we might say today, an elephant through a key-hole), a hand to the plough, a man taking your shirt — all these sayings have directness and immediacy which after the turgid verbiage of committee-English is like water in the desert.

When Charles Davis left the Roman Catholic priesthood he referred in *A Question of Conscience* to the long-winded and unconvincing style of Vatican pronouncements. Now the Vatican may err more than some in this respect, but one only has to receive regular items from the World Council of Churches, for example, to know that involved syntax and circumlocutions are staple material in ecclesiastical circles. It is a perceptive comment of Charles Davis that declares this dislike of plain language to be highly revealing.

The message of Jesus is, on the points that most concern us, as plain as a pikestaff — or as plain as a motorway direction sign, to use a more immediately intelligible simile. We may not like what Jesus says but we cannot avoid it. This kind of clarity is what the newspaper man is always aiming at; in the words of Jesus he recognises the work of a master.

The man who works with words enjoys seeing them used skilfully in a variety of ways. Chaucer's verse, for example is delightful on account of its coarse gusto, its whimsical asides, its tongue-in-cheek easy manner. Shakespeare we enjoy because we like his exploration of the many levels of human experience. Modern writers like George Orwell, William Golding and L.P. Hartley we also enjoy in a similar way. We like tough muscular argumentative prose; we like languid (or apparently languid) irony. We like innocent lyrics and wicked comedy; we like narrative poems and bathetic poems. We enjoy a range of literary works that in some measure entertain and enlighten us. But in the words of Jesus we meet a quite unaccustomed authority. People enjoyed listening to him, but they also were aware that he was telling them what to do. However much enjoyment there may have been in listening to much that he said, there must also have been a good deal of wriggling and reluctant attention as he told his hearers to change their minds and to alter their ways, as he told them to think again and look at matters from a new angle. In short, Jesus spoke as one who knew what he was talking about, and this kind of authority is unmistakable in a press conference or in a written work.

The person who has sought for ultimate truth and has noticed these elements in the Gospels knows that there is something tough and enduring at the heart of Christianity. Shakespeare could invent men with all too credible weaknesses; he could not invent a credible man who was all strength. In the Gospels we come across a unique person who was credible and yet strong all through. We cannot dismiss this figure as a kind of rudimentary superman, a Batman before his time, a magician

171

or wizard who confounded simple people with his sophistries and conjuring tricks. When Glendower boasted of being able to call spirits from the vasty deep, Hotspur could calmly reply, "Why so can I, or so can any man;

"But will they come when you do call for them?"

a reply that demolished Glendower's pretensions. But Jesus was not so easily demolished by flippancy or urbanity. There is an authenticity about the Gospel account that defies explanation. We cannot accept that a man or men could have invented this person. The limited range of a man's imagination would have betrayed him; he would have fallen into absurdity or sentimentality. The story holds together; it does not fold up under critical examination.

It is this which is the ultimate guarantee of Christianity. Beneath the jargon and clap-trap of institutions, beneath the pomp and pageantry and the dull mumblings of committees, beneath the antiquarianism and escapism, beneath the unending stream of words, beneath all that camouflages the essential truth and all too often turns aside the earnest inquirer is a compelling figure who spoke honestly, clearly and with undeniable authority. This enigmatic, commanding, self-contained figure had a purpose of his own which even his closest friends could not penetrate; he set his face resolutely towards Jerusalem to suffer and be rejected on behalf of all men. It is this which men must consider when they are thinking about the claims of Christianity. If men could invent such a person, then Christianity is of no importance whatsoever. If this person transcends man's imaginative capacity and represents an example of human goodness and love beyond what man could conceive, then honest inquirers must seriously consider commitment to him. The authenticity of this baffling central character of the Gospels is the decisive question about which every man must make up his mind — and this kind of authenticity can only be judged in the light of one's own knowledge of what is meaningful and enduring in one's own experience.

Of course it is no answer to Mr Allegro to say that Christianity is affirmation, not speculation. Mr Allegro has set a question-mark against our right to affirm and retain our intellectual honesty, and we have to defend that right. We have to show that it is possible to remain a reasonable human being and still believe in the orthodox Christian faith. But there comes a moment when the Christian must say whatever views others may hold, he himself has found that far from being a symbolic mushroom, Jesus is a living Saviour and Lord. Jesus, the Christian must say, makes a difference to life. When we say this we set ourselves alongside the enormous number of men and women, some notable, most inconspicuous, who have found purpose and depth in commitment to Christ. The Jesus who dealt adroitly with his questioners and pricked the bubble of conceit that his friends all too often carried around with them is one who awakens dormant abilities, engages loyalty and inspires service today as he has done throughout all generations. More than that, he is recognised by his friends and believers as a King, as *the* King. What the Byzantine artists sought to capture in mosaic is the commanding nature of the ascended Christ. For the believer he is not merely the teacher of Galilee, the healer of Capernaum, the quarry of the high-priests and the one who came back from the dead; he is the King of glory − and the devotion of his present-day disciples is more than tinged with trepidation. When the Christian has finished his discussion and argument about Jesus, he knows that he must kneel before the ascended Christ and drive to work under his all-seeing eye. The Christian aims to keep his end up in discussion with the non-Christian as he is bound to do, he hopes that in the process of discussion the non-Christian may modify his views and come nearer to faith in God, but the Christian knows all the time that what

Christ thinks about him is far more important than what he thinks about Christ. The Christian can never talk about Christ as though he is dealing with a specimen in a laboratory; he is always conscious of the life, the ultimate, originating life that there is in the ascended King.

In a sense, then, it is vain to attempt to defend traditional Christian belief. When the evidence has been examined, when the arguments have been arrayed, when the two opposing cases have been put, the choice is not left to sheer logical deduction. Christian faith is not the mere endorsing of a logically demonstrable position. The argument shifts and veers from one generation to another. At one time the argument turned on the nature of Christ's person — was he truly man and truly God? At another time the argument was about creation — did God make the world in seven days or has the world resulted from a big bang? At another time the argument turned on man himself — was sex at the root of all his emotions or was there some ultimate moving power stronger than sex? Now we have to face the question — was Jesus in fact the Son of God paying a fleeting visit to the earth to rescue its inhabitants from their plight, or was he no more than a fictitious by-product of a group of fertility worshippers who could not wait to get on with the serious business of munching mushrooms? Christians recognise that alongside all the arguments one way and the other is a choice between accepting on the one hand the scale of values gropingly sought out by the Greeks, painfully observed by the Hebrews and haltingly honoured by European civilisation and on the other hand a scale of values little better than those of the crudest fertility religions going back to the dawn of history. The decisive factor in making this decision is the person of Jesus. If we find in this mysterious personage something surpassing the inventive capacity of man's mind we shall have to stand abashed in the presence of what we recognise to be supernatural.

It is the kind of reaction that we have when we consider such a person as da Vinci or such a building as St George's Chapel, Windsor, or such a mountain as the Matterhorn. We feel ourselves belittled, dumbstruck, awed. We know that we are in the presence of someone or something incomparably greater than we had imagined possible. This is the intangible factor that compels belief in the man who considers the Christ of the Gospels. Authority, dignity, sublimity — however we describe it — we know that we must defer to a quality and an integrity that humble us and still our chattering tongues. It is a case of "He hath a daily beauty in his life that makes me ugly", but on a much larger scale.

The position then is this. We have what we have always been content to regard as an authoritative revelation from God to man in Christ. Difficulties of interpretation there have always been, but the uniqueness of Jesus has been recognised throughout the ages. Now our attention is directed towards what looks like a series of tired puns to be found throughout the New Testament. It is as though a man has been driving a high-performance car and has found it not only satisfactory but an inspiring machine to handle. One day it is brought to his notice that the name of the car is an oblique allusion to the companions of Odysseus who turned their backs on their homeland and preferred to live at ease in a foreign land. It is also brought to the owner's notice that the tyres of his car bear a reference to a primitive method of making a spark, that the light-bulbs bear a name meaning "lover of horses" and that the name of the oil he pours into the engine contains a veiled reference to the demi-god Castor. Would such a man be well advised to stop using his car and to declare that he would have no more to do with it? Would he not do better to remember the performance of which it is capable and to consider the car as a whole rather than names and labels here and there? The same applies to Christianity. Faith in Christ not only gives meaning to a man's life; it inspires him. For Christ's sake young people cut the toe-nails of destitute old men in the crypt of Spitalfields church, volunteer for missionary service amongst South American Indians, and knock on the doors of strangers during evangelistic campaigns. Whatever puns may be attributed to the biblical writers the overall message "Christ Jesus came into the world to save sinners" makes deep and lasting changes in the lives of those who receive it.

Must we stop being . . .?

... does it really matter in the twentieth century whether the adherents of this strange Judaeo-Christian drug cult thought their community ethics valid for the world at large or not?

John M. Allegro, *The Sacred Mushroom and the Cross*

Against the kind of attack launched by Mr Allegro the traditional defences of Christianity are useless. There is no point in citing contemporary writers like Suetonius, Josephus and Tacitus as providing evidence for the actual life and death of Jesus; we shall be told that Suetonius, Josephus and Tacitus were all alike mistaken; Mr Allegro's myth-makers succeeded only too well. It is the enormity of Mr Allegro's theory that makes it so specious. Arguments for the existence of God are of little consequence if the only god that exists is a phallic symbol in the sky. Arguments about the historicity of the Gospels are irrelevant if the Gospels were written only to provide a vehicle for esoteric punning. At the end of the day we have to recognise that since Mr Allegro has made a kind of pre-emptive strike at the available material the matter has to be decided upon a basis of probabilities. Is Mr Allegro's explanation or the traditional one the more probable?

In the post-Allegro age, we are to understand, the Christian has no right to believe in a God who has revealed himself, in a Son of God who died for man's sins, and in a Holy Spirit who gives men new purpose and life. These ideas are nothing more than elaborate misunderstandings. Whatever good may have been done by men who believed in Father, Son and Holy

Spirit through the centuries of the Christian (i.e. the pre-Allegro) era was the result of a misconception. All that religion could aspire to in the ancient world was a more or less crude fertility cult. The heavenly penis impregnated mother earth. All religion was an elaboration of this. It was ubiquitous fertility that savoured of the divine. Wherever there was increase of man, beast or plant, in that place whatever god there is was active. Particularly was he active in the mushroom, the mysterious fungus that erected itself after rain, the divine seed, had been showered on the receptive earth. There was nothing more in it than that. The ancient myths all point in that direction. Our forebears contemplated the mysterious cycle of birth, growth, death and rebirth; they knew no higher religion. All that we Christians can claim to believe is nothing more than a ludicrous distortion of these environmental examples. A man will learn more about whatever god there may be by reverently regarding the mating of sparrows, or the birth of a foal, or the last gasp of a gun-dog than he will ever learn by listening to the sayings of Jesus or the letters of St Paul.

We Christians must renounce our creeds and confessions now that the post-Allegro age has dawned. Instead of stating our belief in redemption by Christ's blood, instead of holding out our hands for the bread and the wine, instead of singing praises to Father, Son and Holy Spirit, we must be mute and attentive to the works of nature. If we are sufficiently alert, we may come to understand what fertility cult worshippers understood thousands of years ago, that ethical and social values derive from an understanding of the balance of nature. We must not presume to believe that God has made his will known. We must recognise that forgiveness and generosity are not virtues we should cultivate because they are the attributes of God Almighty; they are virtues to be cultivated for the simple reason that it is qualities like these that make it

possible for families and tribes to live together peacefully and ·
fruitfully. The idea that God has anything at all to do with
this kind of pattern is a cock-and-bull story that has by some
freak of history been allowed to determine the history of
Europe. It is high time, says Mr Allegro, that this freak was
exposed.

In exposing the freak Mr Allegro is outrageously specific.
He does not shrink from bringing low the most sacred
elements in the Christian faith. The name of Jesus, he says, is
nothing more than the name of Dionysus (or Bacchus).
The two have merely developed in slightly different ways in
different languages. The crucifixion is nothing more than a
piece of persiflage concealing information about fertility
mysteries. The Holy Communion is a garbled counterpart of
the consumption of fly agaric by its devotees. Christ himself
(he never existed, of course) represents the mushroom; his
crown of thorns represents the remains of a prepuce; his
purple robe represents the tip of a penis. His cry of dereliction
on the cross is merely the appropriate incantation to be used
by those removing the fly agaric from the ground.

Mr Allegro is telling us Christians that we must in all
honesty cease to believe the things we have always believed.
What, for his part, does he believe? He believes, as we have
said, that for nearly two thousand years the authentic message
of the New Testament has been lost to view. He believes that
that message is now revealed in a series of puns involving either
the Greek words of the New Testament or the Aramaic words
that are thought to underly the Greek text. He believes that
the authors of these elaborate puns chose the words they did
because their etymological meaning was significant. He believes
that speculative reconstructions of Sumerian words are an
adequate basis for a revolutionary reinterpretation of the New
Testament. He further believes that a corps of cryptographic
public relations officers concocted a tale convincing enough to

deceive the Roman intelligence system, numerous succeeding generations of Christian people and the vast majority of learned men who have investigated the New Testament since it was first written. Mr Allegro believes that this enormous campaign was mounted in order to do no more than to pass on the name of the supreme fungus. This is not all that Mr Allegro believes. He believes that when well-known ancient writers used the words paeony, chicory, hellebore, mandrake and cannabis, they were all the time intending to refer to the fly agaric; somehow they were confused in their plant lore.

One has to stop for breath after outlining the Allegro creed. What Mr Allegro believes, he believes against all probability, in the face of all the calumny that will inevitably come his way, and on the evidence of his own researches alone. He has allowed philology to shape his views without regard for common sense. Yet his philological reconstructions are on his own confession speculative; they can be nothing better until much more is known for sure about Sumerian and allied languages. If his philology is speculative, his botany is suspect. He is a little too ready to find the fly agaric lurking behind all the plant-names of the ancient world, a little too ready to make the botany fit the theory propounded in the name of philology. He will not be surprised if only a few decide to adopt his beliefs in preference to those that have survived the centuries.

It would be churlish to ignore or depreciate the years of work which are indicated by the notes in Mr Allegro's book. But it would be foolish to overlook the fact that Jehovah's Witnesses practise a similar dependence on a restricted number of biblical texts and that they too secure their position by propounding a novel view about so fundamental a doctrine as that of the Trinity. It would be foolish, too, to overlook the fact that sexual allusions can be found in any literature, and that the man looking for phallic symbols need do no more than step outside his own front door and walk along the street, past swollen-topped lamp-posts and red-topped pillar-boxes. As for the art of the herbalist, every schoolboy knows that here is a subject so intricate as to verge on the occult. Innumerable religions could be built on the bewildering variety of herbs. Emetic, purgative, narcotic, febrifuge: each offers a way of salvation — salvation by vomiting, by evacuating, by drowsing or by cooling. It is by by chewing the root, by swallowing the tincture, by inhaling the fumes, or by munching the dry leaves that the unhappy human will attain to wholeness of life. The aphrodisiac is but one among many vegetable means of attuning the body to the infinite.

If we concede Mr Allegro's points, what are we to make of the rest of the Bible, the part that contains no explicit statement, hint or allusion about the mushroom? The Bible is a big book. Admittedly on Mr Allegro's interpretation the prime event in the New Testament, the crucifixion and resurrection of Jesus, is dismissed out of hand. But there remain the teaching of Jesus and the actions of Jesus. The stories of the Good Samaritan and the Prodigal Son are of self-authenticating excellence; it is impossible to conceive any worthwhile scale of values that would regard them as mediocre. The same is true of the teaching of Jesus. There is wit, crispness and illumination in his teaching and repartee. In the Old Testament there are the insistent demands for justice, the promises of consolation, and the poetry of the prophets. There is the delight in God that we find in the Psalms. The history of David and the other notable characters of the Old Testament is regarded by Mr Allegro as of dubious historicity, but even so there is an immense quantity of material that demands a judgment when the so-called mushroom material has been excised. We have to decide whether this material is valuable, enlarging, and whether it corresponds to the best that

183

man knows elsewhere. It is a matter of judgment. Those who are prepared to dismiss some of the most valuable and meaningful words ever written in favour of a group of fertility worshippers who formed a kind of underground movement amongst the children of Israel are throwing away a diamond necklace (with some of the stones missing, it is true, after Mr Allegro has handled it) for the sake of picking up baubles won at a fair-ground. Mr Allegro cannot be surprised if we prefer to keep the diamonds – all of them.

It is the enigmatic, awe-inspiring, commanding figure of Jesus that we have to set against the specious claims of the mushroom theorists. It is possible to imagine an earnest man coming to the conclusion that God if he exists must be great, good and creative. By doing this he is expressing in general terms the notion that God is better than he is. But it passes credibility to suppose that the best intentioned man could invent the person of Jesus. The mushroom worshipper who was capable of such an act of creative imagination is a man who surpasses Homer, Virgil, Dante and Shakespeare rolled into one. He has contrived to represent a person who has carried conviction in every generation and in every corner of the globe. And – this is the crunch – he has done this as a blind. All this imaginative resourcefulness has been employed to throw the authorities off the scent. The writer has no honest regard for this creation of his; it is meant merely to serve as a piece of paper sculpture in the shop-window.

So much for the Gospels. What of the rest of the New Testament? Mr Allegro finds mushroom symbols and allusions in Revelation, but who cannot find symbols to suit his own purposes in a book which is a show-case for symbols? On Acts and the Epistles Mr Allegro is strangely subdued. Were the deceivers running out of steam at this point? Were they losing their touch? Or was the latter part of the cover story handed to apprentice deceivers who could provide back-up material once the important work had been done. Or — another possibility — was the latter part of the New Testament (excluding Revelation) written by people who actually believed the cover story, so that in effect the mushroom worshippers had their job done for them by the first victims of their deception? Mr Allegro refers to Paul being blinded on the Damascus road by a bright light and suggests that this may have been an illusion caused by the taking of fly agaric. Was Paul then a mushroom worshipper and are the epistles attributed to him as much forgeries as the Gospels? Or was Paul a fictitious character invented, like Jesus, to carry a weight of mushroom mythology? Mr Allegro does not tell us.

Mr Allegro considers the religion of the Old Testament and accounts it man-made. Prophets mumble or scream not the word of the Lord but the result of their latest trip into the wisdom of the underworld. With infinite care man improves and polishes the cultic performance that ensures abundant crops and prolific livestock. With no word from his creator, with no instructions from the manufacturer, he stumbles on his weary way, trying first this, then that, discovering that the one sure consolation in all his troubles is the unchanging, unfailing fly agaric. When the crops fail and the lambs are stillborn, the fly agaric proves not merely an incitement to fertility but a way of escape from the harsh circumstances of the so-called fertile crescent. Man enjoys brief snatches of bliss and longs for more. When he becomes troublesome and belligerent as a result of an overdose of his panacea, he is belaboured by his superiors. They, not knowing the fearful secret that is his, drive him to practise his cultic rites under cover.

Entirely different is the view that looks upon the Old Testament as the story of the education of a chosen people by their creator and deliverer. A weary rabble in the wilderness, a dispirited people in the face of the Philistines, a complacent and contemptuous people under the kings, the Israelites found

185

that whichever way they turned, they could not escape the unflattering progress reports brought to them by the prophets of God. When they felt like giving free rein to their sexual appetites, the voice of the prophets (which must have sounded uncomfortably like the voice of God even to the most hardened profligate) made them think again. When they felt like making alliances with the idol-worshippers around them, they were warned of the consequences of turning their backs on the living God. Even though the Israelites threw out one prophet after another and attempted to silence the voice of God, they could not entirely avoid the warnings of judgment to come. When the prophet himself was silenced, his words were still with the chosen people, on the scrolls that bore witness to the one with whom they had made a covenant.

The orthodox Christian believes that Christianity is a supernatural religion. Whatever fertility worship may have been going on in and around the Holy Land during the time of the exodus, the prophets and the monarchy, whatever strange forms of worship were in vogue amongst Canaanites, Philistines and the rest, among one selected race there was not only a set of sacrificial procedures by which men could receive pardon for their misdeeds; there were some clear instructions about the manner of life that ought to characterise them. Elijah and Elisha are incongruous figures if they are regarded as spokesmen turning a blind eye to sacred prostitutes. Amos insisting on the rights of the poor is a strange partner in erotic initiation rites.

It is possible that the Old Testament is a picture of a muddled and confused situation. It is possible that what we have recorded is a kind of moving picture of the developing life in a duck-pond, with all kinds of creatures finding their way to the top and the strongest surviving. The scene then is one of aimlessness, an absence of co-ordination and a haphazard sequence of events. But it is also possible that the Old

Testament records the deliberate and persistent activity of God in making himself known to the people he had brought out of Egypt. It is also possible that the laws that he gave and the sacrifices that he required fostered in the Israelites a developing sense of responsibility which, despite defeat, exile and dispersal prepared some of them at least for the coming of God's Son. If there are indications that the Old Testament is a muddled and confused record of the activities of many groups, including mushroom worshippers, there is a weight of evidence to suggest that the Old Testament has a unity and a punch that cannot be accounted for by random attempts by men to improve their approach to the fount of fecundity.

Many people today are content, no constrained — and this despite a reading of Mr Allegro's book — to accept the biblical revelation that we human beings have been made by a personal God who enjoys being creative in the way that an artist enjoys achieving effects with colour and proportion. God cannot but be creative; it is part of his nature. Many people are happy too to accept the Ten Commandments as they accept the manufacturer's instructions provided with a new piece of equipment. God has provided us human beings with general directions which, if kept, will enable us to be more truly ourselves. But when we who believe these things consider our own failure to conform to the manufacturer's intention, when we see ourselves proving a disappointment to him, we realise that something must be done to put matters right. We ourselves are hardly in a position to do so — any more than a high-performance car could put right a defect in its own systems. We need outside help. The outside help is provided in God's Son, Jesus Christ, who became man, lived a high-performance human life and gave himself on the cross to meet obligations which we were unable to fulfil. This in brief terms is the message that has put harmony and meaning into jangled and empty lives, has sent the Salvation Army marching into the slums and inspired a man like Dietrich Bonhoeffer to return to Nazi Germany in 1939 to work with the Confessing Church until he was finally hanged in 1945. Countless inconspicuous people would affirm that faith in Jesus Christ is the mainspring of their lives. I call to mind a young teacher and his wife who take themselves and their guitar to countless services and meetings and have regular Bible study meetings in their home. I think of a young salesman and his wife who gladly open their flat to a crush of young people after a youth service and after clearing up the wreckage look forward to the next such occasion. I think of an experienced teacher who spends most of her Easter holiday not recuperating in readiness for the rigours of the next term but organising a children's holiday campaign. I think of an export manager who gives hours each week to his Boys' Brigade company. The list could be extended indefinitely. None of these people would say that they were doing anything remarkable; they believe in Christ themselves and would like to see other people believing in him; they are ordinary people whose lives have been given another dimension by Christ.

The Christian religion is something given, not something invented and elaborated by men overburdened with the importance of fertility. It is in the givenness of Christianity that an orthodox believer must first take issue with Mr. Allegro. Christianity is not so much about the way men have thought about God as the words God has spoken and the actions God has performed towards the creatures he shaped and set on this planet.

Of course we are all tempted to be selective in our handling of biblical material, whether we are Conservative Evangelicals or Anglo-Catholics. It is not for any of us to be too patronising about one particularly able man who has enabled his own pet theory to determine his method of selection. But it must be said that Mr Allegro's principle of selection is so unusual, so

destructive of traditional, catholic belief, so bizarre, so idiosyncratic that we Christians who are busily squabbling over
gnats must beware lest some of our fellows who cannot resist
novelty are persuaded to swallow the camel (saving the word)
that Mr Allegro has put before them.

And what a strange creature it is! If a camel is a horse
designed by a committee, then the camel which we are now all
being invited to swallow at Mr Allegro's behest is the most
curious beast ever to appear on the face of the earth. If
Mr Allegro is right, then the great minds and thinkers of the
Church through the centuries have been poor deluded nincom-
poops. Athanasius, Augustine, Aquinas, Basil, Bernard, Bene-
dict, Calvin, Carey, Clarkson (merely to set the ball rolling)
were men ludicrously deceived into taking the Gospels at their
face value. When they were spending and being spent in the
service of the Gospel, defining the person of Christ, grappling
with the sovereign purposes of God, asking and then answering
systematically all the questions men could think to ask about
God, evangelising the furthest parts of the world, freeing the
slaves, these men − if only they had realised it − were inspired
by a piece of nonsense. They had been bamboozled. They had
fallen into a trap dug for Roman officials by men and women
hooked on mushrooms.

The person who accepts Mr Allegro's theory has more con-
undrums to solve than he had before. If it is difficult to believe
the articles of the orthodox Christian faith, it is even more
difficult to believe that the story of Jesus is really a hotch-
potch of clues about the fly agaric. If it is difficult to believe
that God revealed himself first to the Jews, then in his Son, as
he revealed himself nowhere else, it is even more improbable
that a religious faith that has satisfied generations of discerning
men should have been an inadvertent by-product of a group of
religious drug-takers. Baffling it may be to make head or tail of
some parts of the Bible; it is even more baffling to sort out the

parts written by the punning mushroom men from the parts written by their opponents. The man who has faith in Christ as his Saviour and King will rightly be chary of a novel theory that bristles with baffling improbabilities as does Mr Allegro's theory. With the greatest respect for original philological work and for an imagination that might have been better employed elsewhere, orthodox Christians must say that they are not convinced by Mr Allegro and that the King of glory retains not only his glory but the allegiance of his subjects.

When somebody complained to George the Second that General Wolfe was mad, the King replied, "Oh! he is mad is he? Then I wish he would bite some other of my generals." If a man under the influence of, or out of devotion to, the fly agaric could dream up what we call the Gospels, then we need more men under the influence of the fungus. If the drugs contained in the rind are so potent that they can produce this kind of imaginative power, then all we need do is administer the drug widely and wait for the inspired (or envenomed) poets, composers, painters and sculptors to turn in their masterpieces. Instead of restricting the drug to members of mystery cults, we should persuade as many as possible of our talented people to make use of it. What treasures may be unlocked in the worlds of music, poetry and painting if only existing perceptions are heightened! On a lower level, what may the drug not do for those facing academic examinations! A drug that gave one or more of its devotees the power to hoodwink a whole world for a thousand years or more is a drug that can surely work wonders when rather lower levels of performance are required.

If a man will believe this he will believe anything. Nothing is beyond credibility if Christianity is no more than a mischievous smoke-screen put about by men and women addicted to muscarine and atropine. To have kept the secret is an astonishing enough performance. To have camouflaged it with something as lofty, as commanding, as authentic as the Gospel of Christ argues heights of moral excellence in drug-takers that have never been equalled. by less indulgent men. This world may be a crazy jumble in which the brightest prizes go to the most assiduous mushroom-eaters;.but there are other options, among them orthodox Christianity, with the belief that Jesus was the Son of God, who died, rose and ascended for us men. To believe this is more reasonable than to accept Mr Allegro's hypothesis.

Much more evidence will have to be forthcoming on the philological and botanical fronts before Christians budge from their beliefs. If his views are greeted with scepticism, Mr Allegro will doubtless not be surprised. Christianity has been around for a long time. It is difficult to imagine it being sent packing by a red-topped mushroom at this late stage.